Unleashing Your Leadership Potential

Unleashing Your Leadership Potential

Seven Strategies for Success

Edith Luc

Rowman & Littlefield Education
Lanham, Maryland • Toronto • Plymouth, UK

Published in the United States of America
by Rowman & Littlefield Education
A Division of Rowman & Littlefield Publishers, Inc.
A wholly owned subsidary of
The Rowman & Littlefield Publishing Group, Inc.
4501 Forbes Boulevard, Suite 200, Lanham, Maryland 20706
www.rowmaneducation.com

Estover Road
Plymouth PL6 7PY
United Kingdom

British Library Cataloguing in Publication Information Available

Library of Congress Cataloging-in-Publication Data

Luc, Edith, 1953–
  Unleashing your leadership potential : seven strategies for success /
Edith Luc.
    p. cm.
  ISBN-13: 978-1-57886-874-2 (cloth : alk. paper)
  ISBN-10: 1-57886-874-2 (cloth : alk. paper)
  eISBN-13: 978-1-57886-923-7
  eISBN-10: 1-57886-923-4
  1. Leadership. 2. Self-actualization (Psychology) I. Title.
HD57.7.L814 2009
  658.4'092–dc22   2008025221

∞ ™ The paper used in this publication meets the minimum requirements of
American National Standard for Information Sciences—Permanence of Paper
for Printed Library Materials, ANSI/NISO Z39.48-1992.
Manufactured in the United States of America.

This book is dedicated to my former students, working all around the world—making policy, making trouble for tyrants, making dreams come true—in short, making the world a more hospitable place for people and other living things. They have been and continue to be my source of inspiration and of hope.

Contents

Introduction

For too many, leadership is understood as being a consistent ability of an individual to exert an influence over other members of a group, organization, or domain of activity in a relatively stable fashion. This suggests a conception of leadership in which any given group or social situation can contain no more than one leader, and in which this leader's influence is exerted vertically.

This mental representation of leadership creates certain expectations in our collective subconscious regarding the attributes of a leader who will emerge in a given situation and provide the guidance and the direction or even rescue us. Thus, the image of the leader is elevated to that of a heroic, even godlike, individual, an image from the past. This heroic leader does not exist in reality, thereby causing a high level of disappointment and cynicism when the supposed hero is found to be a mere mortal.

In recent years, however, a number of researchers have attempted to give more consideration to the dynamic aspects of leadership and to consider it as an activity shared between the members of a team, group, or organization, much like communication (Avolio, Jung, Murry, & Sivasubramanian, 1996; Bennis & Heenan, 1999; Pearce & Conger, 2003; Seers, 1996).

Shared leadership is a shared process by which influence occurs, both laterally and vertically, within teams and groups possessing the authority, legitimacy, or power to make decisions (Pearce & Conger, 2003). This definition of leadership as a dynamic process is becoming increasingly important in our various complex, knowledge-based organizations, founded as they are on various forms of teamwork. In our organizations, formal authority is by no means the only source of influence, or the sole method of problem solving and decision making. Multiple views of leadership are present, formal and informal authority, appointed and emergent leadership, transactional and transformational, and each one is necessary, considering needs and contexts.

With the shared process view of leadership where everyone is invited to influence, mobilize, and contribute, it becomes necessary for each and every individual to develop leadership capital and exercise leadership behaviors in areas under our responsibility and act as a leader in our own right by fulfilling the various functions of leadership such as clarifying goals and direction, motivating and mobilizing colleagues, bringing individuals together, solving problems, challenging groupthink and status quo, planning, anticipating future scenarios, freely expressing a point of view, supporting the development of others within the group, and resolving conflict situations.

This notion of leadership as a shared process of influence and meanings presents a new paradigm, not only in the theory of leadership but also in its practice (Drath, 1998), and requires new approaches to leadership development programs.

Each of us possesses—to a varying degree—a potential for leadership that can be further developed, much in the same way that we have a basic physical form that we can improve upon. My purpose in writing this book is to provide the means to unleash the unique capital of leadership inherent in each of us, so that—individually and collectively—we lead our lives, take a more active role in our democratic societies, and improve the lives of others. This book proposes a model for the actualization of the leadership capital that exists within each of us and within groups. Teams and organizations can draw from it to develop their collective leadership efficacy.

Actualizing our own leadership capital means developing this capacity to take responsibility for our own life and the well-being of others. The model doesn't list the qualities to be a leader, but it rather states strategies to develop our own unique leadership capital, with our own characteristics. It aims to encourage more people to exercise leadership, whether in teams or throughout our communities.

The actualization of this capital will benefit both you and the groups to which you belong: families, teams in the workplace, schools, communities, organizations, and others. Without calling formal leadership into question, it nevertheless seeks to make leadership accessible to anyone in a situation where he or she has a contribution to make.

But how do we actualize our own leadership potential? How do some individuals who are not expected to become leaders end up becoming just that? By what different paths do leaders come to take on leadership roles? Are there common denominators in this range of different career paths? If so, what are they? Is it possible to stimulate the emergence and development of leadership qualities in someone else?

The proposed model is inspired by leaders who, a priori, had little opportunity to take on leadership roles in their context for a number of reasons: age, culture, background, education, personality, or gender. Leaders throughout Europe, North America, and Asia provided interviews and observations data. This model is also the result of other observations I made in the course of consulting work within various organizational environments. Finally, two groups, each composed of 35 high-level directors from various cultures—one of which met in November 2002 at INSEAD (a European and Asiatic management school) in Fontainebleau—shared their views on the model produced. Over the years, the model has been the founding basis of many organizational leadership development programs.

The model presented in the following pages, therefore, is based on the life and career paths of at least 150 men and women. These individuals are involved in various spheres of activities, such as business, community work, finance, marketing, engineering, and the manufacturing and public sectors.

WHAT IS NEW AND DIFFERENT ABOUT THIS MODEL?

In the wealth of existing literature on leadership, there are countless studies (for a review, see Bass, 1990; Northouse, 2004). Many are aiming at understanding the emergence of leadership and identifying the followers' characteristics and the qualities required in different contexts, situations, and cultures; others are describing the different styles of leadership; and some others seek to predict leadership variables in employees' satisfaction and performance. Other publications are biographical and autobiographical accounts detailing the paths taken by different leaders in order to explain the individual journey of the leader in question.

Some other authors examine the skills a person must develop to be a leader, taking into account the various preconceptions we have regarding what constitutes effective leadership. This literature, therefore, places its focus on the skills required to perform effective leadership. Some of these skills and qualities include strategic thinking, global vision, problem solving and complexity management, the ability to take risks, emotional intelligence, courage, integrity, humility, motivation, interpersonal communication and teamwork, building and maintaining partnerships, public relations, the ability to reach a consensus within a group, and many more.

Other authors have examined the different strategies organizations use to develop leadership skills, and their results. The most frequent strategies used are on-the-job training followed by formal in-class training, self-knowledge activities, mentoring, and coaching. These leadership development strategies are designed to help managers develop their full potential. They are offered in the form of initiatives within an organization itself or provided by external suppliers of training programs, such as specialized educational or training institutions. The central theme of programs such as these is the development of the skills needed by individuals once they are in a management position.

Being now in a predominantly knowledge-based industry, business leaders and educators are researching ways of encouraging leadership in all those involved in the day-to-day activities of their organizations, rather than targeting only those occupying formal positions of responsibility. Nevertheless, leadership development programs are still offered only to a limited number of individuals, most of whom already occupy managerial positions of some sort.

The model presented in this book, however, is not a study of the skills needed for leadership; rather, it presents seven strategies and underlying actions by which anyone, manager or not, teacher or student, employee or community volunteer, and even teams, can use to free latent leadership capital and then continuously improve it. It is a series of development initiatives that the reader can take up autonomously, in conjunction with formal training and development programs or not. My goal is to make accessible to the largest number of people the strategies facilitating the emergence and use of leadership capital, so that the shared process of influence is activated and the well-being of individuals, teams, and communities is increased.

No other author I know of has proposed a model for leadership actualization accessible to everyone, a model that makes individuals and groups responsible for the actualization of their own leadership capital. Again, most texts on the subject of leadership development refer more to the characteristics to develop or to structured development programs to participate in.

BOOK OUTLINE

The leadership actualization model is developed along seven main lines of strategies, each of which is given its own chapter:

1. Breaking free from social conformism
2. Developing leadership self-efficacy
3. Developing a T approach to learning
4. Building leadership resilience
5. Seeking leadership developers
6. Developing a personal vision, a purpose
7. Getting into leadership actions and engagement

The overall model is presented in figure I.1. The following is a brief outline of each chapter.

The first chapter shows how social conformism is the very antithesis of leadership capital actualization. The social codes of behavior existing within basic groups and organizations all too often prevent the expression of different views and perspectives. The leaders I encountered and studied over the years are all individuals who have gradually learned to distinguish themselves from the various groups to which they belong. By doing so, they gradually freed themselves in various ways from the constraints of the social codes existing within these groups.

This was something they gradually learned even before taking on leadership roles. Breaking progressively free from social conformism allows us to gradually feel comfortable when differentiating ourselves from the other members of the group, to approach and solve problems differently, to deal with social adversity, to take risks, and to stand up with courage and speak honestly. This chapter illustrates the ways in which an individual can break the code of conformism through five driving forces of liberation from social conformism: evaluating the risk of conforming, identifying personal values as opposed to those of the group, developing feelings of personal security, valorizing new social codes, and committing to improve the overall well-being of the group.

The actualization of leadership capital is achieved progressively by building continuously leadership self-efficacy, defined as belief in one's capacity to demonstrate the leadership behaviors required to produce performance in specific situations. Those self-efficacy beliefs impact on decisions to take, effort deployed, perseverance, and success (Bandura, 1977). Self-efficacy beliefs can be developed and reinforced progressively. The second chapter contains strategies for developing and reinforcing leadership efficacy beliefs at both the individual and collective levels.

This third chapter illustrates the "T" approach to learning and the contribution that this makes to leadership actualization. The T approach is an attitude, an effort to develop the depth (vertical axis of the T) and the breadth (horizontal axis of the T) when someone undertakes a task, a job, or a project. The approach is explained in detail in this chapter. Four categories of learners are also identified: passive learners, generalists, experts on content, and those adopting a T approach. Some strategies are also proposed to develop a collective T learning approach to enhance collective leadership.

Resilience in the face of adversity is clearly a characteristic of many leaders, and indeed of all those who face adversity for the sake of their belief in what they are doing or who they are. In the fourth chapter, we see how resilience is required to build leadership capital. In particular, we look at the different varieties of adversity presented by external opposition, internal adversity, and even the surrounding facility. A model for developing this resilience is also presented. The main lines for development of resilience stem from four key areas: personal, interpersonal, professional, and social.

Leadership actualization also occurs through contact with certain individuals who exert a leadership developer role. In the fifth chapter, we take into account six important roles that can be played by these different actors: the mentor, the coach, the challenger, the passeur, the role model, and even the anti-model. Anyone wishing to aid leadership development could benefit from an understanding of the roles played by these different actors, and anyone wishing to develop his or her own leadership capital can pay more attention to those developers.

What meaning and goal do we give to our life? The answer to this simple question is by no means an easy one. However, finding it is essential to encourage individual and collective leadership to flourish. Based on the study of various leaders over the years, the sixth chapter provides an overview of the role that personal vision and values play in the actualization of our leadership capital. A typology of visions, along with corresponding issues, is also provided. The categories include community-based, professional, organizational, supraorganizational, fundamental, distinctive, and generative visions.

Figure I.1.   Leadership Actualization Model

A vision, a project without action, is no more than a wish. Acts of leadership, or shared leadership for that matter, require that every individual acts in any given situation according to his or her own reasons. Aspiring leaders are those who realize that their person, with its inherent strengths and weaknesses, is unique and that they have a worthwhile contribution to make for the benefit of the group as a whole. The seventh chapter presents how getting into action, taking up challenges, and seizing opportunities is key to developing our leadership potential. It discusses barriers to action and engagement, providing strategies to overcome these.

WHO WILL BENEFIT FROM READING THIS BOOK?

Firstly, this book will be of great benefit to anyone who has to exercise formal, emergent, or shared leadership: professionals, teachers and all sorts of educators, change agents within organizations, managers in all types of organizations, political and community leaders, members of teams. This book can also be used in the field of leadership studies and training. Teachers, tutors, parents—that is to say, all those involved in the development of leadership in our society—will also benefit from reading this book. Anyone wishing to develop his or her own leadership capital, and that of colleagues or team members, will also find important lessons here.

Our society needs the contribution of all those who, by their efforts, have the ability to improve the well-being of our local and global communities and organizations. By illustrating the main lines for development in assuming a leadership role, I hope to encourage and support the actualization of this leadership capital and make it accessible to as many individuals as possible.

In writing this book, I wanted to leave behind the usual discussions on this topic and present a different facet of leadership, looking at its potential for actualization and at the inherent potential that lies within each individual. This central theme occurred to me in the course of my meetings with those leaders whose potential would never have been suspected, even by themselves, at the beginning of their adult life. By examining their actions and thought processes, I have been able to identify certain common denominators that can be used by others in a number of different situations.

In writing this book, my hope is to bring about a democratization of leadership. The model proposed in this text runs contrary to the abundance of existing literature on this topic, which treats leadership either as an intrinsic quality or as a set of skills that can be put into action only by a select few individuals.

ACKNOWLEDGMENTS

Writing this book was for me both a privilege and a pleasure. It was a privilege because of the numerous individuals and teams that I have met who were so generous with their time and stories. It was also a pleasure because of the friendly and professional support that I have received from my family, friends, students, clients, the publishing team at Rowman & Littlefield Education and, none the least, my translator, Peter Divers.

I would also like to acknowledge my colleagues and clients for their insights on leadership development. The contribution of people like Laurent Lapierre from HEC Montréal, my friends and colleagues at the Université de Sherbrooke and at the Collège de Montréal, and my clients from diverse companies such as AbitibiBowater, Alcan RioTinto, Avid, Michelin, and SGF, to name but a few, has been instrumental in building the different perspectives in the book.

I would also like to extend a special thanks to my family—Michel, Jean-Alexandre, and Maxence—for being there and supporting me.

By sharing with you the lessons gathered from so many sources, I hope you will experience the same pleasure I had in writing the book. I also hope it will give you the urge to unleash that leadership potential that our modern society so desperately needs to improve our common and small world.

1

Breaking Free from Social Conformism and Leadership Actualization

If man makes himself a worm, he must not complain when he is trodden on. — Immanuel Kant

A social code acts as an unwritten manual for behavior. It defines the rules within a group, specifying what is acceptable or not. Behaving in accordance with this social code helps the group to function more smoothly. However, the downside is that it can easily lead to social conformism, groupthink, and even blind obedience. To develop our leadership potential, we need to free ourselves from detrimental social conformism.

Leading is about influencing, mobilizing, sharing meaning, defining with others new perspectives on goals, finding creative solutions, taking a risk, promoting change. It goes hand in hand with being able to challenge the status quo. Leading is about evolution, progress, and sometimes revolution. Individuals, groups, and organizations all too often are conformists not doing much to disturb conventional ways of thinking and doing, fearing uncertainty and change itself, repression, or rejection. But leadership involves breaking free from social conformism.

The list of leaders who have, at some point in their lives, broken out of the conformist culture surrounding them is a long one. By doing so they were able to lead change and improve the lives of others on top of fulfilling their own dreams.

Because of their decision and initiatives to step out and do or say something to alleviate a situation, they started a change process with positive and sometimes unforeseen results. Recall for a moment the well-known examples of Rosa Parks, Gandhi, or Franklin Roosevelt, who, each in his or her own way, stopped a mainstream view and decided to behave otherwise. Rosa Parks, by refusing to give up her seat to a white passenger, became "the mother of the civil rights movement" against racial discrimination (Academy of Achievement, 1995). Gandhi, by peacefully challenging a British monopolistic law on the production of salt, started a movement to earn Indian independence, and to do it nonviolently (Fisher, 1962).

Breaking free from social conformism doesn't only mean disobeying abusive laws. It can also imply challenging the attitudes of the majority. Roosevelt (1933) did just that when, during his first inaugural address, he coaxed his compatriots to defend themselves from their own fear, their social abdication to hopelessness during the aftermath of the economic depression: "The only thing we have to fear is fear itself—nameless, unreasoning, unjustified terror which paralyzes needed efforts to convert retreat into advance." This statement, this saying at a crucial moment, shook up the people's sense of despair and led them to a better future.

In the education field, this is divergent thinking that inspired Edmonds (1982) to refuse the Coleman Report (Kiviat, 2000) conclusion that socioeconomic background is more significant in predicting child learning than the school environment or the teachers' efforts. According to Lezotte (2002), Edmonds and other researchers set out to find schools that were serving the poor and where children were learning. Their research pointed to a set of characteristics, referred to as effective schools correlates, that served as the basis for the Effective School Movement. Their refusal to conform to a growing conception about school performance led school administrators and teachers toward looking at ways to improve the culture of a school and the achievement of its students. It propagated hope and willpower.

In the business world, it was this capacity that Jack Welch was expecting from employees. Early on, Welch reinforced the need to move GE from a bureaucratic organization that comforted itself in the status quo. He succeeded at shifting the corporate culture and employee mindset, from a bureaucratic one to an entrepreneurial one, alert and ahead in the face of competition (Welch, 2001).

COLLECTIVE AND INDIVIDUAL EXPRESSIONS

Freedom from social conformism can be expressed not only by singular individuals but also by groups of different sizes and even communities. This is the case with three Innu who in 1979 broke from their group's rampant social status and rules, transforming the community from a dejected one to an inspiring one.

The Essipit community, one of the nine communities composing the Innu Nation, once known as the Montagnais, has a success story to tell. As related by their chief, Denis Ross, in 1978 three young Innu university students in their early twenties were discussing their future and their career but also how they could improve the well-being of their society (personal communication, December 6, 2006). Poverty and weak governance were facts of life; the majority of members were unemployed, uneducated, and living in poor housing conditions.

As for many others, the easy choice was to leave behind their native village and start their career in an organization likely to benefit from their newly acquired academic training. Their wages would be quite assured. They decided to do otherwise. They decided to join their forces together, their will and their know-how, and to improve the community's quality of life.

Setting themselves free from both their own community's status quo and collective helplessness and also from their university's peer groups at the time, they started a shared leadership process that would change forever their community and become a source of inspiration for others.

As a result of their initial discussions, the three young friends consulted all the community members, approximately 300 people, thus starting a dialoguing practice. Their objective was to get ideas and a collective understanding of needs, priorities, and aspirations. They then discussed the consultation's results with the community, clarifying the goal to pursue together, and making sure everyone was following the same line of thought.

Their collective purpose, their shared mission, became to do whatever was necessary to bring pride and respect to their fathers and children. They then embedded their community's ideas and suggestions in an operational action plan. The first action was to build a community center where people could meet, share ideas, and take decisions. Since 1978, they follow and update their action plan on a regular basis.

Located on the edge of the St. Lawrence River, the Essipit community grew to be a prominent one, leaving behind a status of poverty and a sense of shame. It is now financially successful, has an almost nonexistent high school dropout rate, and is self-reliant with a full employment rate. Essipit has become, in less than 30 years, one of the most dynamic aboriginal groups in Quebec, Canada.

The community now owns and operates many recreational installations as well as fishing activities and a fish processing plant. They are owners of the grocery store, the police station, and the regional radio, and even have a landscape and a gardening enterprise. To work within one of their businesses, employees have to have at least a high school diploma.

Thus, a major trigger of these three friends' leadership actualization was freeing themselves from the social conformism of their own community and the negative image reinforced by outer groups. This is what Gandhi did when disobeying and opposing British rule in India, or what Rosa Parks did when she challenged the municipal law by refusing to give up her seat to make room for a white passenger. Contrary to popular beliefs they didn't do it all of a sudden. They progressively did it until the breaking moment.

For example, Rosa Parks explains that she was tired of "having to adapt to the byzantine rules, some codified and others passed on as tradition . . . that reinforced the position of blacks as something less than full human beings" (Shipp, 2005, para. 10). In her autobiography, she clarifies further the reason behind her disobedience:

> People always say that I didn't give up my seat because I was tired, but that isn't true. I was not tired physically, or no more tired than I usually was at the end of a working day. I was not old, although some people have an image of me as being old then. I was forty-two. No, the only tired I was, was tired of giving in. (Parks & Haskins, 1992, p. 116)

BREAKING FREE FROM SOCIAL CONFORMISM: THE FIRST STEP TO LEADERSHIP

The ability to gradually free oneself from the grip of social conformism and undue obedience is an important starting point on the road toward leadership actualization. It is also an ability that can be learned, as Rosa Parks, Gandhi, Churchill, and other leaders did when preparing themselves to gradually be assertive, speak up, and stay resilient in face of adversity, opposition. As Gandhi said, "First they ignore you, then they laugh at you, then they fight you, then you win."

In the following pages, the roles of the various existing social codes and the driving or transforming forces that can allow us to free ourselves from social conformism are examined. I then present a number of strategies that can be used to liberate us and others from the shackles of social conformism and actualize our leadership capital.

Organizations, Groups, and Their Social Codes

Human beings are, by definition, social creatures living in groups in order to satisfy their needs for protection, affection, security, access to resources, acceptance, or to contribute something to society. Human society is the sum total of a number of smaller groups, each with their structures and informal social codes. Individuals are categorized first by age and gender (Linton, 1955). They are then broken down into smaller groups: families, ages, clans, or districts, determined by descent, geographical or religious grouping, or various other bonds. They are bound also by shared interests of different kinds: voluntary (groups of friends), work related (professional organizations), political (political parties), for the good of the community (voluntary work), or leisure related (sports and social clubs).

All of our human behavior is deeply influenced by contact with the society, groups, and culture within which it develops. It is through these basic human interactions that the social codes in a society evolve. These codes define the standards of behavior a given group expects from its members. While each individual is capable of thinking, feeling, and acting independently, this independence is nevertheless limited.

Every group, family, scholastic association, professional organization, and religious community has its own codes that are superimposed on the other codes existing within society. Individuals even tend to marry partners belonging to more or less the same social group as their own, and with whom they share similar rules and values (Bonterms, 2001).

Composed of rules and standards, values and beliefs, these codes must be adhered to by any individual who wishes to enjoy the benefits of belonging to the group: emotional or economic protection; access to food or shelter; gaining employment, acceptance, or consideration. Those who infringe these rules are judged by those around them in a number of ways: rejection, expulsion, denial of access to various resources, or other punishments. Adherence to social codes allows society to function and maintains social order.

However, respecting social codes—or social conformism—also has some disadvantages for the individual who, deliberately or not, subconsciously or consciously, obeys them. Social conformism can mean losing touch with one's individuality and aspirations. Submitting to the will of a group can lead to serious errors in judgment, resulting in ludicrous decisions. Social conformism doesn't only have its costs; it can also degenerate further, leading to absurd decisions and, worse still, the loss of human lives (Martel, 2002). In extreme cases, this need to conform can become pathological. There are historic cases such as those who obeyed Hitler.

There are daily and more frequent examples around us each time we or others decide to be silent for fear of being wrong, ridiculed, disapproved, or retaliated against.

In one particular case, a company sought my help following a complaint by three employees regarding psychological harassment by their manager. I eventually discovered that these individuals had set up an informal code of abusive interpersonal and work-related behavior over a period of seven years, which gradually led to the group's members giving in to the demands of its dominant members. The few not conforming were subjected to derision, coarse language, threats, and social rejection.

Organizations provide strong social codes. Managers, clients, unionized employees, union representatives, suppliers, and partners are also key agents in the establishment and development of these social codes, which are supported by incentives such as promotion, economical survival, and various other rewards.

Social Conformism and Risks

While it is important to follow certain codes of conduct because without them chaos would rule, it is also necessary to break free from them when it is needed, when ethics are at stake, and in order to unleash our leadership. Some social codes (or parts of them) can represent all sorts of risks and blockages to a better life not only for us but for others when they reinforce the status quo, when creative solutions—which usually stem from divergent views—are unable to emerge, or when entrenched standards and practices damage the integrity of the group, its members, and its stakeholders.

Silence—the main language of social conformism—is too often found within organizations (Perlow & Williams, 2003) and in our society. Silence takes a significant toll on organizations and society in terms of immobilism, restricting creativity, harming productivity, allowing greed and immoral behaviors, and damaging the motivation of its employees when they feel uncounted for, humiliated, bitter, or undervalued. Conformism fossilizes the society's and organization's culture, leaving it too rigid to anticipate and experience change, too hermetic to integrate divergent thinking, and too blind to foresee problems that might cause serious errors.

The Enron disaster is a prime example of the way in which the pressure to conform and the culture of silence among chief executives allowed one a major financial fraud to occur. The leaders within the company with the power to voice their disagreement with these fraudulent practices could have done so much sooner and much more loudly than they did, had their awareness of and freedom from social conformism been greater. There are many other such examples: Parmalat, Everest, Tyco, and WorldCom.

An example that I witnessed closely is that of Allan, who was considered a leader with great potential. Promoted to the post of director for an organization of 880 employees, he gradually conformed to the new management group, losing his critical view and unique perspective on events around him. He slid gently into a pattern of conformism, accepting unquestioningly the management team's views on critical issues.

Allan failed to question, for example, their view that the continuous decrease in the plant's performance was caused by external factors over which the organization had, or so they believed, "no control." His acculturation to the management team and his compliance with its social code prevented him from seeking a fact-based approach to the problems. The situation deteriorated dramatically; the performance results fell behind, and the company lost its reputation along the way. He finally had to resign when headquarters assessed the situation.

Ethics and Breaking Free from Conformism

One of the recurring themes of my interviews with different leaders is their tendency to break the various implicit social codes around them. Their ability to overcome the social consequences of their behavior grew steadily over time, allowing them to build their own confidence in their ability to reject various forms of unnecessary social conformism in a number of different situations.

Developing our leadership means developing the ability to free us to some extent from the constraints of our social environment, to have an awareness of the codes of conduct imposed by the various groups around us, and to decide freely and on our own terms to act differently or to step outside these limits. Just as Rosa Parks did. This can be beneficial not only to us as individuals, but also to the group who, consciously or not, hope for better solutions and conditions.

Breaking these social boundaries doesn't mean breaking ethical or moral codes. It means stepping beyond the social boundaries of the group to take an idea or a discussion forward or in a new direction, to live up to our dreams, to have our rights and needs and those of our groups respected and answered.

The act of freeing oneself from social conformism is an activator of leadership capital since leadership acts require a certain amount of independence and the ability to seize the initiative, defy the status quo, be innovative, give consideration to a new or different point of view, approach problems from different angles, tell the truth while others hold their silence, and, above all, take necessary risks.

This ability to free oneself from social conformism is, therefore, one of the key elements of learning to exercise leadership. Being a leader means having the ability to be aware of the pressure coming from the group around us and yet put it aside and take the risk of expressing an idea, opinion, aspiration, or view.

In other words, breaking the cycle of conformism within a group allows leadership to take place. In order to achieve this, however, nonconformism and even, at times, a certain degree of dissidence and disobedience are required.

Nonconformism and Counterdependence

Breaks with conformism—key moments in the foundation of leadership— are similar to but also different from those experienced by all adolescents in the course of developing their own identity. It is similar when adolescents voice their true opinions and values to their first primary group, which is the family. It is different when adolescents systematically oppose their parents for the sake of it. The latter pattern of behaviors is more counterdependent in nature than a true affirmation of a free choice. Counterdependence is a psychological process by which an individual becomes dependent on an individual or a group as the result of a constant need for opposition.

Breaking free from conformism does not mean being motivated by the desire—conscious or otherwise—for opposition per se; it is motivated by the inner desire to express who we are and what we value or want for ourselves or a group. Counterdependence inhibits just as well the development of the individual's leadership capital.

Society and organizations need individuals with the ability to break these rules in order to progress in the right direction. And, just like our physical form, this ability to step beyond the boundaries of social conformism is one that can be developed. It does, however, require constant maintenance and practice.

DEVELOPMENT STRATEGIES

So how can a member of a group free himself or herself from blind compliance with social codes and the conformism engendered by any group? What can we do to help others to actualize their leadership capital through this process of liberation?

In the following pages, we will examine the release mechanisms that can be used to free us from unnecessary social conformism. But first let's review three basic competencies required to become freer from conformism:

1. Communication skills, such as listening, asking questions, clarifying, synthesizing ideas, and reformulating
2. Assertiveness, or the capacity to stand up for ourselves
3. Negotiation, or the capacity, through dialogue, to get a shared agreement with another party, a person, or a group

These three skill sets permit us to get our idea across and in more and more challenging social situations without being unduly compliant with group's norms. And in developing others' leadership capital, we may want to increase their communications, assertiveness, and negotiation skills. There are numerous training workshops and books on these three sets of competencies.

The first set of competencies has to do with interpersonal communication. It involves the skills necessary to understand another point of view though listening, clarifying questions, and finally validating our comprehension through synthesis and reformulations. The more skillful we are at using these competencies, the more capable we can be at bringing in a different point of view by first acknowledging others' views, and therefore instilling a true dialogue.

Assertiveness is another basic competency associated with freeing us from social conformism. It requires learning to express who we are, our needs, our rights and ideas, and to do it with assurance, without demeaning our interlocutors with aggressiveness or manipulative ways. Assertive people are more likely to break free from inappropriate social codes, being adept at expressing who they are and what they want, self-assured and without fear.

Finally, negotiation skills are the third basic set of competencies linked to getting freer from social conformism. Negotiation involves the dynamic and interactive process of influence. Someone adept at these skills resolves in a more cooperative manner all sorts of disputes from simple requests to important disagreements. Strategies and tactics of negotiation vary from one situation to another, depending on values, what is at stake, and the interactions between those involved.

The object of the next section is a review of five strong motivational forces that can instill a drive to free ourselves from conformism.

The Driving Forces of Liberation from Social Conformism

Different strategies for breaking free from undue conformism can be grouped into five main categories, or driving forces:

- Analysis of the risk posed by conformism
- Identification of personal values versus those of the group

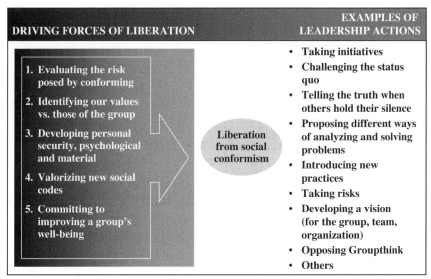

Figure 1.1. Links between Driving Forces of Liberation from Social Conformism and Leadership Actions

- Development of a personal security
- Valorization of new social codes
- Commitment to improving the well-being of a group

Figure 1.1 illustrates different strategies and the potential impact on the likelihood of leadership behaviors.

Analysis of the Risk Posed by Conformism

In any social situation involving a group of people, we usually tend to consider the risks of not complying with a view or a decision. Here, I propose to do just the opposite, meaning developing a helicopter view of the whole situation, by analyzing the risks associated with conforming.

Understanding these risks rather than simply looking at the benefits of conformism allows us to counteract the usual (almost naïve) human tendency to focus on the positive aspects of a situation, person, or future scenario. This analysis of the situation also gives us the impetus needed to take action.

The individual who does this divergent analysis, for example, defining the risks to conform, understands that there are significant risks associated with conforming and that doing so could have serious consequences both for the individual and the group as a whole.

To cite our earlier example, if Allan had seen the risk of conforming, he might have understood the risk posed by maintaining the status quo and would not have ignored to such an extent the poor performance, quality, and morale issues around him. In this way, he might have halted his own downward spiral into conformism. Seeing the risks of conforming would have revealed greater freedom than giving way to the benefits of conforming.

Analyzing the risks associated with conforming to a social or organizational situation is a way for us to expand our leadership potential. Learning to analyze the risks posed by these different instances of conformism brings with it a discipline of independent thought. It also allows the gradual emergence of an individual's leadership capital and influence within a group through a capacity to understand group dynamics.

Identification of Our Personal Values versus Those of the Group

A second driving force to increase our capacity to become free from the constraints of conformism lies in the capacity to know our own values and recognize the gap between them and those of the group. Values can be defined as the beliefs of a person or social group regarding what is important: family, freedom, social cohesion, honesty, authenticity, teamwork, self-discipline, overcoming one's limits. For example, Rosa Parks explains to Greenhaw (2005) that it was her desire for dignity for all that supported her opposition to the bus driver: "I felt a determination cover my body like a quilt on a winter night" (para. 10). Her values gave her the strength to resist.

Individuals unsure of their own values are more susceptible to social pressures, external influences, group pressures, and threats. They tend to get more caught up in the social codes of the various groups around them than those who are firmly grounded in their own system of values. Strong values also serve as a reference point when we are making difficult decisions.

Having solid fundamental values, and a sound knowledge of them, allows us to stand for or against some projects and ideas with greater assurance. Solid values can even bring someone to disobey orders should the need arise. Therefore, being clear on what our values are expands further our leadership capital.

Values are central to any organization. In the hope that their employees be guided in their choices and behavior by certain values, organizations tend to promote core values in their day-to-day activities. By doing so, they build a shared set of beliefs and values, encouraging their employees to have the strength to act accordingly and to resist pressures of some subgroups when their set of values diverges from the core ones.

For example, integrity—the basis for all trust relationships—is one such value that organizations put forward in their code of ethics. It encourages employees not only to live up to this standard, but also to act when others are failing. An individual with a strong integrity basis is better able to dissociate himself from the group, denounce overtly inappropriate behaviors, and even initiate new ones more in accordance with his or her values.

Values such as these are more influential when they are supported by concrete measures within the organization. They carry no weight if those transgressing against it go unpunished, if management fails to take the steps necessary to remedy unethical behavior, or if managers themselves are acting inappropriately.

Therefore, values are a strong driving force to free us from social conformism as long as they are clear and embedded in our individual ethics. You may want to reflect about yours to unleash your capacity for leadership tasks. For instance, you can do that by writing your reflections about your own life-guiding principles, at home, at work, in your community, with your family and friends, with your colleagues, neighbors, or cocitizens. You can determine these through discussions with significant others: a friend, a spouse, a colleague, a relative, a teacher, a coach, or a trainer. Furthermore, as values evolve during a lifetime, you may want to revisit these from time to time.

Developing Personal Security

The development of personal security is another driving force that can free us from social conformism. It is partly the lack of personal, material, or psychological security that causes individuals to conform to the wishes of others. Fear of losing access to resources (power, money, status), fear of being rejected by the group, fear of conflict, fear of losing face or appearing foolish if an idea is not well received, fear of being alienated from the authority figure in the group, and fear of being denied interesting and challenging projects—these are all factors providing a strong incentive to conform.

In the case mentioned earlier, in which the employees kept quiet about the abusive behavior of their colleagues, it was the fear of being misjudged by management and losing their jobs that caused them to hold their silence for over seven years. Those who were more secure in their value or in their ability to get a job elsewhere left the company after making complaints to their immediate superior, who failed to listen and were blind to the situation.

Even in situations not involving harassment of this kind, it still often happens that members of a group do not dare to break the bonds of social conformism for reasons of personal insecurity. This phenomenon of compliance with groups exists at all levels in an organization, even at the upper levels, in the context of board meetings, for example. Ideas emerge and opinions are shared, but they usually tend not to go beyond the boundaries implicitly laid down by the group's social code in regard to controversial ideas.

It takes a lot of determination and self-belief to bring previously unaired or taboo subjects to the meeting table. It is essential to do so, however, if only to bring value-added and sustainable solutions.

There are many ways of developing this sense of personal security, but two key ones have to do with examining our relationship to material security—money and job, for example—and learning to understand our social environment better.

Having debts, in addition to limiting our options (professional or other), has a pernicious effect on personal security. We conform to a group for the sake of maintaining or improving our material situation.

Reevaluating our relationship with money and constantly developing our skills allow us to reduce the influence that an individual, group, or organization can hold over us, therefore giving us more latitude. In short, we must strive to restrain ourselves from acquiring unnecessary debts or financial obligations that don't have a return on the money invested, and develop continuously our skills and competencies so that we can rely on these to expand our options, if our situation changes.

Understanding our social environment better—with its problems, paradoxes, dynamics, and unspoken rules—allows us to increase our confidence in taking the right direction or bringing a supplementary or complementary point of view to the table. It provides us with the capacity to recognize better, and more rapidly, what is at stake in any given group.

In short, the secure individual will be better equipped to deal with the risks that accompany nonconformist behaviors than an insecure one.

Valorization of New Social Codes

The fourth main driving force of liberation from the social conformism is the valorization of new social codes, or parts thereof, through the indirect support of individuals or groups for whom we have more respect on some issues than we do for another group. By a process of social comparison in which we compare the social codes of two groups—our own and another—we are able to determine which of the two groups corresponds best to our own values, interests, or aspirations. Valuing the social code of another group does allow us to further consolidate certain aspects of our identity.

The adoption of new social codes can also take place as a result of encounters with historical or biographical accounts of different leaders. Mintzberg (2004) indicates that such biographical accounts represent some of the favorite readings of many leaders. They often draw inspiration from these accounts when later faced with important decisions to make. With the help of some texts, the reader can grasp new views of the world, reinforcing the development of new perspectives.

Another way to value new social codes is by exposing ourselves to different cultures that will provide us with a lifelong conviction that there is more than one way to live our life, more than one view of (or perspective on) solving problems. This intercultural exposure frees us from the constraints of our original social code (i.e., family, region, school), and makes us more flexible by giving us the agility to approach problems and solutions from different angles. An intercultural exposure legitimized some of the nonconformist decisions and actions of many of the leaders I met. Their new social code became a hybrid of their own original code, thanks to their contact with various cultures.

The valorization of new social codes, therefore, presupposes a certain level of openness and a willingness to learn from others.

Commitment to Improving the Well-Being of a Group

The fifth force driving us to break free from social conformism is developing a belief that we can or we must act for the good of a group. This feeling also allows us to develop a vision for the future of the group and to commit ourselves to work toward it.

The importance placed on the well-being of a group, not necessarily the one immediately around, gives an individual the strength of will needed to overcome taboos, forbidden topics, and conformism, if not comfort. In order to do this, in my view, two forms of social intelligence must be developed: a restrictive social intelligence and a collective social intelligence.

Restrictive social intelligence refers to the capacity to understand what is taking place in a restricted group, in the immediate group such as a family or team, with regard to its functioning, its needs, its expectations, and the social pressures its members are subject to. By grasping the dynamic of the group, its standards, conventions, needs, and expectations, the individual can behave more freely. Otherwise, the person is caught up in the intricacies and emotional turbulence of the group. Furthermore, the results of this social intelligence (such as understanding and management of the group dynamic), when shared with the members of the group, make it easier for the group's members to learn to work together as a team.

Collective social intelligence is related to a larger group such as an organization, a district, or a community group. Collective social intelligence brings with it an understanding of the needs and workings of a larger social ensemble and the recognition of which collective needs we can or should contribute to. This second form of social intelligence is essential to being able to provide the best possible leadership in serving the collective interest. Furthermore, the desire to improve the well-being of the group as a whole frees us by making us less self-centered.

This ability to effectively free oneself from social conformism will develop only through use in increasingly demanding social situations.

Table 1.1 presents some examples of nonconformist behaviors:

Table 1.1. Examples of Nonconformist Behaviors

1. Achieving higher standards of performance than expected.
2. Refusing the negative image of yourself sometimes projected by colleagues, friends, or parents.
3. Studying in an unconventional area (domain). Studying, living, or traveling outside your own country.
4. Establishing a different career path from classmates and colleagues.
5. Developing unconventional interests.
6. Taking on new responsibilities or projects, regardless of objections from others regarding age or prior experience.
7. Developing and implementing strategies for improving customer service or product quality, despite the opinions of colleagues, immediate superiors, or groups within the organization.
8. Developing a community program despite lack of initial interest from others (e.g., those with decision-making power).
9. Disobeying orders when called for in situations of abuse or lack of integrity.
10. Being among the first to accept organizational changes despite initial resistance from the majority of your colleagues.

CONCLUSION

Society needs positive leaders—regardless of gender, ethnicity, or training—who are capable of improving the lives of others. In today's knowledge-based industry, and the flat world (Friedman, 2005) where the complexity and speed of decisions continue to grow, leadership is needed outside the boundaries of strictly hierarchical structures.

Leadership must be deployed wherever important tasks require the ability to influence a group over which no vertical power can be exercised (e.g., citizens, elected representatives, politicians, suppliers, clients, or colleagues). But to ensure that leadership emerges from a larger number of people, men and women have to be encouraged from an early age to lead their own lives, contribute to a collectivity, and leave behind the apparent comfort of conforming quietly to their familiar groups.

Remaining silent and submitting to group thinking are telltale signs that an individual has fallen into the trap of conformism. Educators and parents have to give people the freedom to show and celebrate their differences, ideas, and opinions in the way they approach problems and their solutions. Above all, however, they have to encourage them to avoid conformism and groupthink, and to take risks for their own sake as well as for the interests of different groups.

2

Developing Leadership Self-Efficacy

Trust yourself, then you will know how to live. — Goethe

One significant quality shared by all accomplished leaders is their confidence in their capacity to achieve their goals. They believe that, given a certain amount of effort, they will succeed in achieving their objectives. The question then becomes, How do they develop this confidence? We will see in this chapter that leadership confidence or what we can better name leadership self-efficacy beliefs can be developed and that those beliefs impact on actions, effort deployed, perseverance, and success. Strategies to reinforce individual and collective leadership efficacy beliefs are presented.

At the end of the 1960s a young Portuguese woman, aged 17, immigrated in France to join the rest of her family and help them make ends meet. Maria Fernandez (personal communications, May 17, 2000, and September 11, 2002) had only a basic grasp of the native language. Before long, she worked as a waitress in a restaurant but also as a maintenance worker in a small firm specializing in commercial and industrial cleaning. One day, this second employer offered her the challenging job of supervising a team of 15 employees.

Thinking that she was not the right person for such a position, she intended to turn it down. But her current employer convinced her that she was capable of succeeding in this role and that she shouldn't hesitate but accept the challenge. This simple and sincere response proved to be a major turning point in her life. She took up the challenging opportunity and gradually took roles of greater and greater responsibility within the company, building stronger and stronger beliefs in herself and in her leadership capacity.

Thirty years later, she found herself, alongside its founder, at the head of Penauille Polyservices. This business, specializing in industrial cleaning and airport services, had more than 38,000 employees; its operations spanned 200 airports in 40 countries. During the course of my interviews with her, Mrs. Fernandez highlighted the importance of these signs of trust in the actualization of her leadership capital through the confidence-building effect it had on her.

Laurent Beaudoin, the main driving force behind the success of Bombardier Inc., the railway and aeronautical manufacturing company, confessed to me (personal communication, January 2002) that, as far as he is concerned, building employees' and future leaders' self-confidence should be a core value of any organization and every education program.

Another example of the crucial role of building strong beliefs in oneself in the actualization of leadership capital is the case of Anne Lauvergeon, current president of AREVA, who is rated by *Fortune* ("Global Power 50," 2005) as one of the most powerful global business leaders. AREVA is a world leader in the energy market, specializing in nuclear energy and electricity supply. As reported in their 2007 annual report (AREVA, 2008), it has an annual revenue of 11.9 billion Euros and according to their website, a workforce of 71,600 employees.

When I asked Ms. Lauvergeon (personal communication, June 21, 2000) which factors were significant in her leadership actualization, she immediately recalled the influence of her grandfather, who made her believe how unique she was. In her child's eyes, he was a very important person. She recalls going for long walks with him at age 10 discussing all manner of things. For example, he would speak with her quite simply and openly about his projects and investments. Receiving so much attention from him was, as she says, an extremely important factor in the development of her self-confidence.

She has also been shown considerable confidence by other important figures in the course of her career. The most notable of these are her first employer, Richard Lévy, former president and director general of Renault, who acted as a mentor.

While she was still in her thirties, Francois Mitterrand, then president of France, offered her the opportunity to join his team, entrusting her with a great deal of responsibility during the General Agreement for Tariffs and Trade (GATT) negotiations. She thought it was well over her capacity, and at first refused this responsibility. In the end, and after much hesitation, however, she accepted this important opportunity. She remembers her first few months in the job being highly stressful and demanding. The media even questioned her ability to succeed at this level, considering her relative youth. It was at this point in her career that she decided to stop worrying about criticism, deciding instead to build on the trust shown in her by others.

She describes herself as an average student at high school to pinpoint the fact that she didn't consider herself being more capable than others, exceptionally intelligent or talented, but maybe just more self-confident. She believes that it is her commitment to hard work and effort that have made the difference, on top of the trust demonstrated by significant persons.

What can be inferred from these examples, from many other observations with leaders, and from research findings on leadership and self-confidence (Bass, 1990) is that building self-confidence is an important factor in leadership development.

In this chapter, I present strategies for developing leadership self-efficacy. But first, a distinction between self-confidence and self-efficacy is described.

CONFIDENCE AND SELF-EFFICACY
IN LEADERSHIP ACTUALIZATION

Tens of thousands of texts have been published on the subject of leadership over the past 50 years. Though abundant, this body of literature remains far from conclusive on a number of points, most notably with regard to the specific attributes possessed by leaders. This is probably due to the fact that leadership can be exerted in an infinite variety of situations requiring an array of different characteristics: personality traits, aptitudes, values, interests, competencies, and so on and so forth.

Nevertheless, researchers and authors in this field have at least pointed to the importance of self-confidence (Northouse, 2004) and assert that "self-confidence is a necessary trait for successful leadership is undisputed" (as cited in McCormick, 2001, p. 23).

Moreover, whether Japanese, American, Canadian, or French, research carried out by GLOBE researchers (House, Hanges, Javidan, Dorfman, & Gutpa, 2004) across different cultures and contexts has supported a similar conclusion. One of their findings points to being decisive, the behavioral side of self-confidence, as a key element contributing to outstanding leadership (Grovewell LLC, 2005). Consequently, leaders must demonstrate confidence, a belief in their ability to achieve their goals in the situations in which they find themselves and despite any difficulties that may arise. But what is self-confidence?

Self-Confidence

Self-confidence can be defined as a fundamental, stable, and general personal belief in our value. It is a positive, basic, and steady appreciation of ourselves regarding our general capacity.

In organizational settings, confident supervisors will be more inclined to engage in discussion with their subordinates than to issue orders (Bass, 1990); they rely less on administrative rules and coercion, and they act in a more decisive manner than managers with less self-confidence.

Interviews, coaching, and observations of leaders over the years have allowed me to pinpoint that most of them didn't have an initial view of themselves as "born leaders." They expanded their leadership's initial capital by constructing stronger and stronger leadership confidence or self-efficacy beliefs through experiences, observing and learning from models, encouragement from others, and a constructive attitude toward self as well as toward successes and failures.

Leaders have built their leadership self-efficacy through experiences, and at each stage of leadership actualization.

Self-Efficacy

Self-efficacy is related to self-confidence and self-esteem but with a difference. As specified by Bandura (1997), self-efficacy is a judgment of "one's capabilities to organize and execute the courses of action required to produce given attainments" (p. 3), while "confidence is a nondescript term that refers to strength of belief but does not necessarily specify what the certainty is about" (p. 382). Self-confidence is less precise, less specific than self-efficacy.

Self-efficacy beliefs are related specifically to a certain set of situations; they are beliefs in one's capacity to demonstrate the behaviors required to produce designated levels of performance in specific situations. For example, one can have high self-efficacy beliefs to demonstrate the behaviors to succeed at a given sport but low self-efficacy beliefs to demonstrate the behaviors to succeed in another sport.

Self-efficacy is the central theme of the theory presented by Bandura (1977, 1986, 1997). It has been shown to be an excellent basis for predicting the outcome of a wide range of performance-related situations: sports, academics, phobia treatments, sales, rehabilitation, and others.

> Such beliefs influence the course of action people choose to pursue, how much effort they put forth in given endeavors, how long they will persevere in the face of obstacles and failures, their resilience to adversity, whether their thought patterns are self-hindering or self-aiding, how much stress and depression they experience in coping with taxing environmental demands and the level of accomplishments they realize. (Bandura, 1997, p. 3)

Self-efficacy beliefs determine how people feel, think, motivate themselves, and behave (Bandura, 1997). The stronger these beliefs are, the more likely the individual is to make the effort required in order to succeed. Conversely, the weaker self-efficacy is, the less effort the individual is prepared to expend and the more likely it is that he or she will fail in a given situation (Bandura, 1977).

People who doubt their capabilities shy away from certain tasks and are less committed to their goals. When faced with difficulties, they dwell on their personal deficiencies or on potential obstacles, rather than concentrating on the best way to perform successfully.

In addition to the sense of personal well-being it brings with it, self-efficacy also allows individuals to invest more of their time in learning and developing the skills needed in a given field. Consistently reinforcing self-efficacy not only results in improved performance but it also gives the feeling of being in control of our own lives.

People draw on four main sources of information in order to gauge their self-efficacy beliefs in whatever field of activities (Bandura, 1977). These sources of information result from

1. Personal experiences, thus the need to live direct experiences of progressive difficulty.
2. Observation of others in action.
3. Verbal persuasion of others and other types of social influences. This is where coaches, allies, and mentors play a key role (see chapter 5).
4. Emotional responses to events as they happen. Emotional responses such as fear, stress, or satisfaction give us information about our vulnerability and state of anxiety and can influence our self-efficacy.

The most interesting aspect of the theory of self-efficacy is that self-efficacy beliefs can be developed, thus giving access to a whole range of learning possibilities including leadership behaviors.

Leadership Self-Efficacy Defined

We can define leadership self-efficacy as the judgment one holds regarding his or her capacity to execute successfully leadership behaviors that will bring desired outcomes of influence and mobilization toward a common goal.

When we stop considering leadership as an immutable inner quality, reserved to born leaders, and see it as a shared process of influence and mobilization, we can then start the interesting voyage of engaging ourselves in developing our capacity for leadership behaviors, since these leadership behaviors can be exemplified by everyone, not just hero type persons.

We can build continuously our leadership efficacy beliefs, and consequently our capacity to influence, mobilize, and contribute.

The benefits of expanding our leadership capital are numerous on top of seeing oneself learning and developing continuously. Besides an increased ability to successfully influence and mobilize others, it improves the feeling of being in control of our own lives. It increases the capacity to contribute to improve the life of others. Finally, it provides the likelihood of getting positive feedback and encouragement from others regarding our contribution, actual and potential.

Leadership self-efficacy is essential to leadership actions, but not only that, it is a necessary condition for succeeding.

Therefore, the first step to unleashing and developing leadership is to step out and exercise any of the various behaviors of leadership in your own context, considering also that leadership actions are as diverse as the situations we find ourselves in, and that learning has to take place in leadership situations of progressive difficulty, not being too easy or too overwhelming.

As self-efficacy is related to behaviors, table 2.1 offers an illustrative list of leadership behaviors so you can target specific ones to exercise.

You might not encounter success every time you exercise leadership behaviors, but you can become better at doing it only by practicing leadership actions. Be aware, however, that explanations you will give for your performance can strengthen or weaken your leadership self-efficacy. For example, blaming a poor performance on a lack of intelligence or "talent" will be detrimental to reinforcing self-efficacy beliefs, since these are factors over which we have no control. The best route is to look for factors

Table 2.1. Examples of Leadership Roles and Behaviors

Roles
- Being a board member of a lucrative or a nonlucrative organization
- Leading a team
- Leading a project
- Leading an organization or an association
- Leading or initiating with others a neighborhood project: cleaning, recycling, building a sport facility, and so on
- Leading or initiating (with others) a school project: parent-teacher activities; welcoming day or week; career week; recreational activities; end of school celebration; conferences on parenting, managing homework, and so on
- Accepting or looking for the next level of management responsibilities
- Others

Behaviors
- Voicing an idea, an opinion, an analysis and perspective of a problem to another individual, a team, or a larger group
- Promoting change to another individual, a team, or a larger group or to opponents
- Clarifying goals, purpose, or objectives
- Encouraging others to participate
- Giving positive and constructive feedback
- Challenging the status quo
- Proposing constructive solutions while maintaining positive relationships
- Integrating different points of views in a solution
- Others

within your control such as efforts deployed prior to and during the leadership situations encountered.

Based on research findings in regard to self-efficacy, and on my personal observations with experienced leaders, the next section proposes strategies to develop leadership efficacy in yourself, in others, and in groups.

STRATEGIES FOR DEVELOPING LEADERSHIP SELF-EFFICACY

Developing Your Leadership Self-Efficacy

How can you develop leadership self-efficacy in order to strengthen your own leadership capital? These strategies are set out in table 2.2 below. They are grouped into five main categories:

- Taking up challenges, in situations and in larger projects (experience mastery).
- Better knowing yourself in order to focus on strengths, talents, interests, and areas for improvement.
- Employing constructive cognitive strategies to reinforce constructive mental processes and reduce detrimental ones.
- Continuously developing know-how to build competence, bring value, and increase influence.
- Leveraging constructive social influences by developing allies and collaborators and being inspired by models.

These strategies are detailed below.

Taking Up Challenges of Progressive Difficulty

The best strategy for developing leadership self-efficacy is to live up to leadership experiences by placing oneself in leadership roles or by exerting leadership behaviors in different situations. Usually leadership opportunities abound throughout our social environment once we finally understand that leadership doesn't only happen at the head of an organization but that it is a shared process of influence and mobilization.

Table 2.2. Strategies for Developing Individual Leadership Self-Efficacy

Strategies	Corollaries
1. Experiences • Taking up challenges, in situations and in projects.	• Challenging experiences of progressive difficulty develop leadership self-efficacy, as long as you attribute success to your qualities and efforts, and failure to insufficient effort or difficult circumstances.

2. Self-Knowledge
  • Identifying your talents, strengths, and interests.
  • Forming a life purpose and identifying your values.
  • Identifying obstacles preventing you from improving or enforcing leadership self-efficacy and your self-confidence.
	• Focusing on and investing yourself in your interests or talents increases your chances of success.
	• A life purpose and clear values allow you to give your best in order to achieve these goals and uphold these values.
	• The next step involves taking action to overcome these obstacles.

3. Cognitive Strategies
  • Positive internal discourse: transforming useless, negative self-criticisms into a more positive and constructive discourse.
  • Positive visualization: picturing yourself succeeding, particularly in leadership situations.
  • Openness to learning and experience: treating adversity and challenges as opportunities to learn and increase self-efficacy.
	• Mentally reviewing and repeating the expressions of confidence and trust you receive.
	• Identifying the situations to deal with, then gradually progressing from easy to the more difficult ones.
	• Turning away from the pure pursuit of comfort and materialism, seeking out challenges instead.
	• Succeeding in the face of difficulty makes us stronger.

4. Know-How
  • Becoming the best in your field or profession.
  • Taking on more and more projects that further develop your skills and leadership.
	• Aiming to be the best requires the necessary amount of effort and experiences.

5. Social Influences: Models, Allies, and Collaborators
  • Learning from others displaying leadership roles and behaviors.
  • Identifying and knowing your allies and supporters.
  • Encouraging relationships that build confidence.
  • Discussing with people having different viewpoint from yours.
	• We learn a lot through social learning: encounters, direct observations, meeting different persons and groups, and readings.
	• Being receptive to positive or constructive feedback, to the positive challenges you are given, to encouragement, and to valorization.

Positive experiences of exercising leadership increase self-efficacy beliefs, thus the necessity to experience leadership in progressively difficult situations in order to increase our chance of experiencing success, and to develop continuously our leadership capacity.

Self-Knowledge

Self-knowledge shall be directed at gaining a sense of our own unique value, a key constituent of leadership self-efficacy. As Bass (1990) highlights, "Self-understanding is essential even for the most successful leaders" (p. 152). The path to self-knowledge includes learning both about who we are in general and about our leadership strengths and improvement opportunities in particular.

Understanding ourselves means identifying our strengths, talents, interests, aspirations, and values. It involves also identifying our flaws and our own obstacles to achieving a greater sense of worth. Finally, the process of knowing more and more about ourselves involves reflecting on our experiences and constantly learning from these.

Many strategies can be used to increase our self-knowledge: regular reflection on ourselves, our interests, personal history, and experiences. This can be carried out either alone or with the help of others, through questions and discussions, or by using professional tools such as 360-degree feedback, and psychometric tests of personality and interests.

Cognitive Strategies

Cognitive strategies are strategies involved in the process of thinking, knowing, being aware, learning, and judging. Mental processes affect our emotions, our experiences, and consequently our actions and our performance because of the way in which the brain works.

By using cognitive strategies, we can strengthen or weaken our self-efficacy, or our belief in our capacity to succeed in specific leadership tasks. Believing in our ability to succeed will effectively increase our chance of success and the efforts put forth in order to succeed.

Cognitive strategies for strengthening leadership self-efficacy involve paying attention to our thought processes for the purpose of managing the way by which we mentally process information about ourselves and our social environment.

The most useful cognitive strategies in regard to leadership actualization are control of our own internal discourse, visualization, mental openness to experience and learning, reflection on learning, and mental attention to building and maintaining positive or constructive personal relationships.

Monitoring our internal discourse is an initial strategy of the self-observation process. It involves being aware of the discourse we have in terms of how we value ourselves, how we talk to ourselves before and during performance, and how we account for our success or failure in various leadership situations. It can also involve examining our own representations of what constitutes leadership, and how it affects the way we take up leadership opportunities or not. Being aware of our self-conversations is the first step in managing these.

Keep in mind that any negative view of yourself can only cause feelings of incompetence or inefficacy, which reduce your leadership impact by bearing on the quality of your relationships with others.

You might want from time to time to use a personal notebook where you might inscribe not only your thoughts but the emotions you experience. You will then realize what needs to be reinforced and improved.

Self-criticism is one area that you might also wish to reflect on and improve. Are you criticizing yourself unnecessarily? What are you criticizing yourself about? Whom do you hear when these criticisms assault you? Is this view of yourself a just appreciation? Can you find out by asking others? For example, do you tell yourself that you are not a leader, still holding a utopist view of leadership?

Another way of silencing self-criticisms is also learning to stop criticizing members of your group, team, or organization; you will then progressively learn to see positive sides of people and situations and construct more productive thinking. Seeing the positive sides of people will also develop a capacity to see yourself more positively.

Eliminating these negative thoughts and self-criticism are strategies deliberately adopted by many leaders who had realized that they were doing themselves considerable damage by being needlessly hypercritical of themselves. After all, did Beaumarchais not say, "Stop criticizing yourself; there are plenty of others more than willing to do it for you!"? You might want to recall that sentence when self-criticism is again present in your thoughts.

Managing our internal discourse content involves also paying attention to how we analyze the reasons for any particular outcome. This internal analysis can also be either harmful or beneficial to self-efficacy beliefs. For example, attributing success to luck, and failure to a lack of intelligence or aptitude can reduce your self-efficacy strength because these causes are not under your control. In fact, it can even damage your belief in your ability to repeat previous successes (i.e., without being lucky again). On the other hand, the more successes and failures are attributed to effort (or lack thereof), the greater your self-mobilization and sense of control when facing other similar challenges in the future.

A useful way of analyzing your mental processes is to make notes on your thoughts and emotions over a period of time, a few days, for example. These notes should contain your internal thoughts, phrases frequently present in your mind, and the questions and comments that occur before, during, and after certain leadership situations. In this way, the room given to negative thinking, self-criticism, and other harmful thoughts becomes evident. It is only by becoming aware of your internal dialogue that you can take steps to reprogram it. One of these mental reprogramming techniques is the use of positive or constructive language (internally and publicly) regarding yourself and others.

Effective leaders, through the language they use and therefore the mental representations they provide others with, distinguish themselves by their ability to project an optimistic yet realistic vision of themselves, of the world around them, and of the ability to face the challenges that lie ahead. A study by Zullow, Oettingen, Peterson, and Seligman (1988) on this subject showed "that nine out of the ten losers of presidential elections between 1948 and 1984 tended to emphasize the pessimistic side of issues in their nomination speeches" (p. 678).

Visualization is another cognitive strategy that can be used for leadership development. It refers to the projection of a mental picture of a leadership scenario you hope to achieve. Repeated positive visualization, also known as cognitive rehearsal, allows you to imagine yourself demonstrating the leadership behaviors that will bring you success in increasingly difficult situations. For example, picturing yourself calmly defending a controversial point of view to a colleague or a patron or in front of an entire team will increase your leadership self-efficacy beliefs and, therefore, your actual chances of success when this situation occurs.

When used in tandem with relaxation techniques, this method can prove very effective.

In order to increase leadership capital, the specific leadership situations you visualize are to be targeted and relevant to your current needs, such as defending a point of view, standing up against the status quo, forming a common vision, reconciling divergent points of view, establishing partnerships, negotiating or resolving disputes. The more specific and detailed the visualized situation is, the more effective it will be. Qualified personal coaches can also help with this type of strategy.

Mental openness to experience and learning is another strategy aimed at consciously drawing attention to the importance of being open to learning and, consequently, to leadership experiences. It requires a state of open-mindedness to leadership learning provided by experiences, observations, readings, and reflections. This strategy requires a certain level of self-discipline, a curiosity for learning, and also the ability to listen to those who can improve your learning.

A corollary of this mental training to learning and experience involves the viewing of adversity as a learning opportunity rather than as a series of pointless obstacles. As well as helping in the development of resilience (see chapter 4), this process also allows you to summon the energy you need by gradually building up your confidence in the face of increasingly difficult leadership situations.

Know-How

Being the master of your task or an expert in your field, whatever it may be, is an important part of building your leadership self-efficacy. The support provided by this knowledge base and the recognition it brings with it are crucial to optimizing leadership. Moreover, studies by Joiner and Josephs (2007) on the stages of leadership development identify the first level of leadership maturity as that of expert, where individuals concentrate their time and energy on developing their knowledge and skills, and where their influence is mainly linked to their know-how.

Social Influences: Models, Allies, and Collaborators

As demonstrated by the examples of leaders examined earlier in this chapter, self-confidence and self-efficacy flourish through social learning or contact with others, relationships with colleagues, allies, or role models, and through constructive feedback and verbal persuasion.

Social learning lies at the heart of an entire process aimed at increasing our awareness of individuals who develop our leadership capacity by being role models, challenging us constructively, providing words of feedback and encouragement, and proposing progressively challenging projects and tasks, building on past successes.

Recognizing and nurturing relationships with collaborators and genuine allies requires the improvement of our ability to build strong and significant relationships. When confidence is shown in an individual, it is then up to the individual in question to accept this sign of confidence and appreciate its value.

Social learning involves also learning from the experience of others through readings, encounters, and direct observations, but as long as we compare ourselves positively with these models. Learning by observing others is most effective when we perceive ourselves as similar to the models in some ways. If we want to develop leadership skills, we better learn from models that we consider not only inspirational but comparable to us in some ways.

The factors for comparison are varied and highly a matter of personal choice, such as age, training, gender, profession, common interests, the same values or aspirations, family background, same organization, and even the same flaws. These models provide highly informative comparisons for judging and verifying one's capacity. Models of leaders that are unreachable, with which we can hardly identify ourselves, won't do much, but someone who we consider sharing some similar characteristics or aspirations will have much more impact.

This careful attention to the quality of our social influences and relationships develops self-discipline by improving our ability to discern the quality of various relationships and then to rapidly decide what to do from the following options:

- Make the best of these social influences.
- Determine the actions required to resolve the negativity experienced in some relationships by asserting ourselves; modifying the nature, structure, or frequency of the relationships concerned; and sometimes, even ending them.

- Stop to focus our attention on interpersonal incidents, relationship, or people that drain our energy and reduce our beliefs in ourselves.

The people who damage leadership self-efficacy beliefs are those who constantly criticize or personally attack our beliefs in our ability to succeed and who tend to be contemptuous of our efforts. They should not be confused with challenging colleagues, who actually make a significant contribution to the growth of our self-confidence through their trust in our abilities and talents that their demands indirectly demonstrate.

We achieve the building of efficient relationships, therefore, by bringing ourselves closer to those who increase our self-confidence, managing differently or distancing ourselves from, or at least minimizing the impact of, those who are harmful to it.

We have examined so far strategies to develop our own leadership self-efficacy. Let's now have a look at how to develop it in individuals and in groups.

DEVELOPING LEADERSHIP SELF-EFFICACY IN OTHER INDIVIDUALS

The strength and vitality of leadership within organizations depend as much on the leadership shown at all levels throughout the organization as that at its head (Gardner, 1990).

In every type of organization, there is a strong need for better and more generalized leadership, in political organizations as well as in business ones, in nonlucrative organizations as well as in lucrative ones.

It is also the case for schools where the need to reform schools for better performance calls for stronger and better leadership (Fullan, 2006). But in order to bring sustainable change, not just initial and superficial success, Fullan emphasizes the need for developing leadership of many others in the organization. This will serve the interests of continuity and reinforce collective efficacy.

In today's knowledge-based industry (and throughout society), where educated workers want to feel involved and where the decision making is decentralized in the interest of clients and of the employees themselves, organizational leadership should now be considered in terms of the cumulative effect of every member's and every team's leadership. And in all organizations increasingly structured around knowledge and different specialized teams, the collective and shared leadership is what really happens, where people work together to make reciprocal meaning, create shared goals, and commit to work toward them (Drath, 1998). Shared leadership involves, therefore, the accountability and responsibility of every member to step out and be part of that reciprocal process, thus the need to develop everyone's and every team's capacity for leadership.

Consequently, we need individuals capable of developing leadership in others. This ability in itself constitutes an act of leadership, with leaders developing others in turn. The responsibility for this task is the preserve not only of managers and the members of these various teams, but also of teachers, trainers, and parents. Increasing the leadership self-efficacy of others is a key component of the sustainability of leadership development initiatives.

Table 2.3 presents some of the strategies that can be employed in order to develop leadership self-efficacy in others. These strategies are particularly concerned with

1. Providing experiences of progressive difficulty: varied and challenging, giving more and more tasks that build on acquired competencies while propelling individuals and teams to higher levels of leadership performance.
2. Having high expectations, being demanding on quality and performance, and showing signs of trust in their leadership potential.
3. Continuously developing leadership and content-related know-how by giving access to experiences, training, and development programs.
4. Using constructive language such when providing feedback on leadership situational performance, giving words of encouragement, reminding them of their past successes, and emphasizing lessons learned.
5. Modeling constructive cognitive strategies such as stopping unnecessary criticism, using explanations for performance that are under the individuals' and teams' control (e.g., efforts), providing

Table 2.3. Strategies for Developing Leadership Self-Efficacy in Other Individuals or Teams

Strategies	Corollaries
1. Provide experiences: • Provide individuals and teams with access to a wide range of experiences, with the necessary autonomy to succeed, even when they do not yet have all the necessary experience. • Valorize initiatives and different points of view.	• Don't wait for individuals to be completely ready before offering them new responsibilities, but build on their previous successes. • Give them leadership challenges slightly above their current level.
2. Show high expectations: • Be demanding of people and their work.	• Being demanding demonstrates trust in their ability to achieve the targeted results.
3. Continuously develop know-how: • Provide (give access to) training and development programs related to individuals' and team's work and leadership.	• The first level of leadership maturity is expertise. Training and development programs build participants' confidence and beliefs in their own abilities in their context. This demonstrates, by the same token, trust and respect in people.
4. Use constructive discourse: • Use constructive and positive language. Comment on the progress made and skills to improve. • Demonstrate trust in the future, in the attainment of shared purpose and objectives, in people's capacity to succeed.	• Avoid making negative or devalorizing comments about an individual or a team. • Do not talk about leadership in rigid or deterministic terms (e.g., innate quality).
5. Cognitive strategies: • Stop unnecessary criticism. • Use explanations for performance that are under control (e.g., efforts); provide constructive visualizations of success.	• Your attitude reflects on others, thus the need to demonstrate a constructive and can-do attitude—others get inspired to do the same.
6. Social influences: • Allow individuals and teams to meet with important and influential people and models, for example, the head of the organization.	• Meeting people they consider important allows individuals and teams to increase their own sense of importance and provides them with leadership role models.

constructive and optimistic visualizations of leadership challenges and situations.

6. Providing access to social influences: models, allies, and collaborators.

Developing leadership self-efficacy is as important for a collective, such as teams, organizations, and societies, as it is for individuals. The last part of this chapter on developing leadership self-efficacy reviews different strategies for developing collective leadership efficacy.

DEVELOPING COLLECTIVE LEADERSHIP EFFICACY

A considerable number of texts produced on the subject of organizational performance emphasize the importance of teamwork within our organizations, characterized as they are by their complexity, their speed of decision making, and the variability and the volatility of client and market needs. Therefore the collective sense of efficacy of any team is a key constituent of its capacity to succeed.

But as stated by Bandura (1997), "Although perceived collective efficacy is widely recognized to be highly important to a full understanding of organizational functioning, it has been the subject of little research" (p. 468).

Conceptually, the notion of the collective sense of efficacy is separate from the self-efficacy beliefs that individuals have regarding their personal ability to achieve their goals. The collective sense of efficacy refers to an overall perception among team members regarding the team's ability to perform and succeed together. The collective sense of efficacy is a group-referent perception regarding the combined abilities of a group, organization, or society to do what is required in order to achieve a goal.

In order for a group to engage itself and persevere in the face of obstacles, it is essential that every member not only possesses strong personal self-efficacy beliefs but also a strong sense of collective efficacy, or belief in the group's capability of performing and succeeding. A team's collective sense of efficacy influences its performance within an organization or community. It affects the team's performance not only in terms of achieving its stated goals, but also in terms of the importance that is placed on the mission at hand and, consequently, the degree of effort made by the group. It will also affect the manner in which the members of the group work together and the resilience they show when faced with problems (Bandura, 1997).

A meta-analysis by Gully, Incalcaterra, Joshi, and Beaubien (2002) concludes that the relationship between collective efficacy and team performance is positive and significant. Campion, Medsker, and Higgs (as cited in Bandura, 1997) reported that

> perceived group efficacy, which they call potency, is positively associated with group self-management, flexibility and variety in job assignments, shared purposes and a sense of responsibility for the work, good communication among coworkers, managerial support, and mutual support and sharing of work loads. (p. 448)

Bandura (1997) reports also that "schools in which the staff members have a strong sense of collective efficacy flourish academically. Schools in which the staff members have serious doubts about their collective efficacy achieve little progress or decline academically" (p. 469).

Building on the concept of collective efficacy, I propose the notion of a sense of collective leadership efficacy that I define as a collective judgment of the group's capacity as a whole to influence, mobilize, transform, and impact others, within or outside the organization. Executive teams, project teams, change management teams, HR teams, procurement teams, or any other team whose mission is to transform ways of doing things or lead change all need a strong sense of collective leadership efficacy in order to mobilize their respective stakeholders to achieve a common goal.

The stronger the perceived collective leadership efficacy, the higher the probability of teams, and members of those teams, engaging themselves in succeeding, taking ownership of results, and persevering despite obstacles and setbacks, influencing and mobilizing other individuals, stakeholders, and groups. How to develop a strong sense of collective leadership efficacy is the subject of the next section.

Determinants of Collective Leadership Efficacy

Building on the theory of Bandura (1986), and on my own professional observations in multiple organizational settings, I propose the following determinants of a perceived collective leadership efficacy:

1. Each member's strength of leadership self-efficacy beliefs.
2. The collective competence of the team in regard to their shared common goal.
3. The previous record of success of the group in leading change and projects and influencing and mobilizing stakeholders.
4. The group's status within the organization or perceived importance given by influent members in the organization or society.
5. The positive or constructive feedback from the team leader as well as from other members or groups and feedback regarding the team's capacity for success within the organization or society.
6. A positive and favorable outlook when the team compares itself to other comparable groups or teams.
7. The emotional well-being of the group as a whole when working together. The more difficult and unpleasant the group finds it to work together, the more the feeling of collective efficacy will suffer. The more positive the collective experience is, the stronger the sense of collective efficacy will be.

The ways in which the group accounts for its successes and failures are also important and will affect its collective leadership efficacy. In order to maintain and strengthen the perceived collective leadership efficacy, these explanations for performance (good or bad) should be based on factors within the group's control (e.g., effort and skills development).

Strategies for Developing Collective Leadership Efficacy

The following strategies can be put forward in order to continuously develop a collective sense of leadership efficacy of a team or a given group:

1. A clear shared purpose or collective goal to achieve. The development of collective leadership efficacy is directly linked to the goal

that the group pursues together. Moreover, a shared goal provides the common ground to measure progress made. Positive or negative progress toward a common goal will strengthen or reduce the perceived collective leadership efficacy.

2. Judicious selection of team members (when possible). These members should have the competence, skills, and motivation required to succeed within the context; ideally, each team member should also have a strong personal leadership self-efficacy, or at least be working at improving it.

3. A collective information-sharing process of team members' skills, as well as of their past and current achievements. This information process allows the whole group to gain an awareness of each member's capacity relevant to the mission at hand. This provides the team with a clear view of its strengths and collective competence at the outset.

4. Persuasion of the team's importance and competence within the organization. This strategy involves persuasion and feedback given not only by the team leader but also by the rest of the team and other stakeholders. Every team member should reinforce the same message of trust and confidence to the others and about the team to any other stakeholders. This has the same positive effect on the team's feelings of competence and performance.

5. An action plan to address the collective task at hand and follow-up progress. Realizing progress to make and made gives a sense of control toward achieving a common goal.

6. Opportunities for team members or the whole team to develop leadership skills. This can be done by giving progressively challenging tasks and by a specific leadership development program offered to the whole group.

7. Emotional regulation of the group. Emotional regulation involves the group's ability to manage the emotional aspect of their life together, using for example, and when appropriate, humor, constructive feedback, assertive requests, social activities.

8. Developing resilience. To allow collective leadership efficacy to grow even stronger, the group must take care to develop a collective resilience in the face of problems by focusing on a common goal, continually striving for excellence, developing the collective know-how

of the group, emphasizing the learning taking place, enhancing group cohesion, and even using humor. All of these elements stem from a clear shared vision of the team's defining goals.

CONCLUSION

The development of leadership self-efficacy is an important factor in the actualization of leadership, and it is under our control. This chapter presented strategies to develop leadership self-efficacy.

Our responsibility as citizens, employees, students, or parents is to develop the unique leadership potential that we have so we can cooperate for the benefits of realizing our shared destiny. Each of us can step out and be part of the circumstance in which we find ourselves, and therefore exercise influence.

Given the fact that today's organizations tend to be based on teamwork, developing collective leadership efficacy also merits particular attention.

3

Developing a T Approach to Learning

Those who have achieved success since ancient times began their tasks through attentive work on the smaller issues, for they knew that the building of a small edifice has to begin with its foundation, and a piece of silk of a thousand meters has to be made accumulating the weaving of every thread. —Chinese Maxim No. 2175

To unveil their capacity for leadership roles and responsibilities, leaders I met and studied have undertaken their tasks with a T approach to learning. That is to say, their work is characterized by two basic learning attitudes. The first of these is the effort put out for a profound understanding of the content of the tasks or missions for which they are responsible.

The second element of this approach is their attitude to also broaden their understanding and expertise beyond the boundaries of what is strictly necessary. In this way, not only do they develop an incontestable task mastery, an essential factor in motivating those around them; they also increase their holistic and systemic ability to gain a broader perspective on the problems and their solutions. This T approach is one of the defining strategies to unleash leadership capacity.

T LEARNING APPROACH

How do individuals develop their ability to influence and motivate others around them and stimulate responsibilities in the workplace or for the community? What have they done differently in order to arrive at this point? The answers to these questions (in addition to those already covered in previous chapters) highlight the importance of their learning process from an early stage in their professional lives.

A large proportion of the actualization of their leadership has occurred through a T approach to learning. The first dimension of this attitude is the depth of understanding (knowledge and know-how) that they have developed continuously in their own field or area of responsibility; this represents the vertical axis of the T. It is the sound foundation of their learning. The second dimension is the breadth of their knowledge and know-how in terms of other aspects, directly or indirectly connected to their immediate expertise or area of responsibility; this constitutes the horizontal axis of the T.

It should be noted at this point that the approach to learning taken by these leaders in their professional lives does not necessarily correspond to the type of students they were beforehand. In fact, a number of them were by no means model pupils in their younger days. However, their level of commitment to learning from the very beginning of their professional lives was altogether different. From this point onward, these leaders approached the responsibilities they were given with a real determination to understand every aspect of them. To unleash leadership potential, we need to confront work-related issues in a manner that allows us to develop our own knowledge and know-how constantly, both vertically and laterally.

I would like to give three different and concrete illustrations of a T approach to learning before presenting how to develop this learning attitude, both at the individual and collective levels.

The first T learning case is exemplified by a program developed by the Kellogg Foundation (2007a) to promote collective leadership in communities. Without necessarily referring to this terminology, their program capitalizes nevertheless on associated T learning strategies by

1. Developing participants' collective expertise regarding their own community (vertical bar of the T).
2. Developing what they call social and cultural literacy, namely by providing the participants with the complexities of the community context: its history, culture, demographics, politics, and economics (vertical bar of the T).

3. Selecting participants so the group is composed of a variety of social, economic, cultural, and experiential profiles (horizontal bar of the T).
4. Providing opportunities for them to exchange best practices and resources (horizontal bar of the T).
5. Building understanding horizontally across boundaries so community members open up to new ways of seeing each other (horizontal bar of the T).

Their key principle behind the rational for the leadership development program is that leaders cannot be effective at addressing a situation unless they fully understand the whole picture (Kellogg Foundation, 2007a). As illustrated in the foundation's annual report (Kellogg Foundation, 2007b), their leadership program is quite successful by virtue of initiatives taken and results achieved by communities themselves, such as developing actions to keep students from dropping out of school, and mobilizing youth, families, and communities or forging partnerships between education institutions and communities.

The second example has to do with the initiatives taken by a junior professional in a field yet unknown to her. During a sojourn to India following her university studies, Marie-Claude Peyrache, a former senior executive at France Telecom and now president of the European Professional Women's Network in Paris, was given her first professional contract (personal communication, March 2000). She was contracted by a telecommunication firm to examine the existing level of communications technology in India. At this point, she had no technical expertise to do that, having been trained in economics and business management.

Nevertheless, she did everything in her power to gain a sound understanding of the workings and the state of this industry, and showed no hesitation in consulting the technical documentation available, or in requesting meetings with telecommunications experts as well as with political and economic analysts. She made sure to cover all possible aspects of the current and projected situation. By doing so, she was able to produce an analysis of the situation that exceeded all expectations.

Even more important, however, was the fact that in the course of this project she gained the belief that she could achieve anything she wanted as long as she was willing to invest the time and energy needed to fully understand the various elements of a situation or problem. She had learned to develop a T learning approach, a strategy that enables her to influence and mobilize people in every task and project she undertakes.

A third example of this T approach to learning and its role in activating leadership is that of Dr. Jonathan Mann, an epidemiologist and AIDS researcher. On top of a degree in medicine, Dr. Mann held a BA in history and training in public health administration. His medical work gradually led him to become involved in AIDS research at the time when the disease was just beginning to become more widely known. Thanks to his knowledge and understanding of the medical aspects of AIDS, as well as his deep understanding of the humanitarian, sociological, psychological, economic, and legal issues, he was able to convince and mobilize the world's political leaders to deal with the problem (Hilts, 1998).

His mastery of knowledge about both the depth and breadth of AIDS allowed him to exercise a considerable degree of leadership, notably by making decision makers worldwide aware that ignorance was a key factor and that AIDS sufferers' human rights needed to be better protected. Mann (Fee & Parry, 2008) developed a theory of human rights and health: "His development of a systematic approach to human rights and HIV/AIDS, and later to health more broadly, reflected lessons learned in his early career as well as his experiences directing the World Health Organization's (WHO) Global Program on AIDS" (para. 4).

His efforts led to a concerted effort toward public education and behavioral change. He was the one who, at a world health conference, convinced health ministers to invest in education campaigns. Policies were changed, education programs started to take off, human rights were protected, research took off, and condoms were distributed (Doctors of the World, 2007).

Dr. Mann would never have had the same impact if he had focused only on the purely medical aspects of AIDS.

BENEFITS OF A T LEARNING APPROACH

An active T learning profile helps us to gradually actualize our leadership capital in a number of different ways. Above all, this approach to learning allows developing a firm grasp of the issues we have to deal with, providing us with a broader perspective of the situations, a more strategic way of thinking, clearer decision-making abilities, and a greater sense of self-assurance in general. All of these factors contribute to give a particular value and a thoroughly researched contribution we can make when we deal with problems, challenges, and the needs of other individuals or group members.

In sum, T learning is a process through which learners progressively expand their leadership capacity by building both a deep and a systemic understanding regarding a situation, an issue, or a challenge. It deepens and broadens at the same time the diverse views of the subject, its factors, impacts, and roles. This learning process can only bring deeper and larger knowledge and understanding, as if the T keeps growing along life experiences:

$$_\mathrm{T}\mathrm{T}\mathrm{T}\mathrm{T}\mathrm{T}$$

This T approach to learning requires the effort to gain a deeper understanding of challenges and problems and also to understand the subsystems that may be associated with them. It expands gradually one's capacity to influence and mobilize because of the building blocks of knowledge, understanding, and know-how.

For example, a young teacher can focus solely on the tasks assigned to her such as teaching math. But if she wants to further actualize her leadership capital and her ability to influence not only her class group but the school decision-making process (both now and later in her career), she will have to widen her focus.

She will do so by first mastering her subject matter, then striving to fully comprehend the purpose, the sense, and the impact of her work and its interrelations with other elements of the classroom such as the group dynamics, the students' profiles, needs, concerns, and learning results.

She will then gradually broaden her understanding, paying attention to and eventually acting on her observations of the quality and attractiveness of the physical environment, the organizational culture, the partnering with parents and other community stakeholders, some management issues, or any other issue related to current problems or to education in general (horizontal axis of the T). Her understanding will impact her capacity to propose solutions and influence and mobilize different stakeholders, and all this for the benefits of the students.

This holistic approach toward learning allows the aspiring leader to grasp a problem in its entirety rather than focusing solely on his or her own particular field of expertise. It also enables the person to establish important links between the various aspects of a domain, the classroom, the community, and education in general.

This does not mean that aspiring leaders have to become obsessed with details, or that they have to be experts on every subject. This learning approach simply helps them in carrying out strong and well-anchored leadership actions.

When this learning profile is adopted early, the individual concerned is able to gradually build a strong foundation of knowledge and know-how that will be of great use to a larger and larger group. This method of learning also suggests that leadership capital actualization is accelerated when, within or outside the organization, we step beyond the limitations of our own specific roles to gain an understanding of the larger world we are involved in and our interdependence with others.

Moreover, the authors of Project Globe—an international research organization studying cultures, efficiency, and organizational behavior—conclude from their research in over 130 countries that competence in dealing with the specific task at hand is an important attribute valued in leaders of all cultures (House et al., 2002). According to the authors, being administratively skilled, being informed, and being oriented toward excellence are universally considered as attributes contributing to effective leadership.

T learning is therefore a key strategy in unleashing and building leadership capital. But is this approach to learning something immutable? Where does it originate and how can we improve it?

ORIGINS OF LEARNING ATTITUDES

The different attitudes toward learning can be explained in several ways. Sometimes, learning attitudes are developed through the lens of our social environment; for example, in response to our parental or academic feedback about our successes and failures, or by observing peers' or key models' attitudes toward learning in general.

We gradually interiorize the importance of effort and hard work and gain greater confidence in our own capacities when—as children, students, or new employees, being more or less successful—we are encouraged to work harder or enhance our efforts, and when we are praised or praise ourselves. And the probability of succeeding increases further.

On the other hand, when parents, teachers, or managers, or even we ourselves, blame and criticize our failures or devalue our achievements, there is a risk that we will begin looking for ways to avoid learning situations in order to avoid placing ourselves in these negative situations again. Learning can also be motivated by a fear of the consequences of failure more than an enjoyment of it or the anticipation of its rewards.

Hanna's case clearly illustrates the way in which an individual's social environment (school, family, peers) can shape an attitude toward learning. As a child, her mother punished her severely whenever she failed to achieve the highest marks at school. Her relationship with learning was therefore based on her underlying fear of chastisement, punishment, and even the shame of not being at the top of her class. Her mother passed to her a deep sense of humiliation whenever she was not among the school prizewinners.

Hanna also carried this attitude over into her working life, where her learning and general performance were motivated more by her fear of reprisals than her desire for pleasure or benefits. She still achieved a certain level of success, as she was a competent worker and quite a perfectionist, but her own underlying aspirations and life goals lay elsewhere. Her leadership capital was therefore inhibited by this negative relationship with learning. She couldn't move beyond an expert role in exercising leadership. Fortunately, childhood learning experiences can be overcome depending on the individual's resilience (see chapter 4) and his or her subsequent experiences and motivations.

As educators and parents and even colleagues, we can assist others in their learning process when we address the beliefs that learners have toward specific learning. We might strive to convince them that

1. Learning efforts will yield results.
2. The results themselves (e.g., the pleasure of learning itself, agility, employability, pride, social recognition) are worth the efforts.
3. They have the ability to succeed or the capacity to demonstrate the behaviors required to succeed. Sometimes, this requires breaking down the learning process into tasks of progressive difficulty.

Learning attitudes and beliefs further explain why some leaders, despite being far from model pupils in primary and secondary schools, develop a T learning attitude as soon as they gain an interest in certain studies, professions, or projects.

Another factor contributing to the formation of individuals' attitudes toward learning lies in their sense of responsibility for what happens in their lives, a feeling referred to as the locus of control (Rotter, 1966).

Some people have a fundamental belief that whatever they attain and whatever results they achieve, it is a direct outcome of their own efforts or lack thereof. Their perceived locus of control is therefore referred to as internal. Others believe that these outcomes are most often the result of factors beyond their control such as luck, destiny, circumstances, or the influence of more powerful individuals. Their locus of control is therefore referred to as external. They usually don't feel responsible for what happens to them. Individuals in the latter category put less effort into learning unless they get external incentives such as rewards, salary increments, or social recognition.

According to Rotter (1975), the concept of the locus of control is not a dichotomy, where the individual has either an internal or an external locus of control. It is more like a continuum on which a range of different attitudes can be found, and this continuum varies according to situations and reinforcement expectancy. An individual whose locus of control is generally internal can, in certain situations, attribute success or failure to external factors in other situations. In general, however, individuals tend to have a locus of control that is mostly internal or mostly external.

Up until this point, we have examined the role of a T approach to learning in regard to its contribution to leadership capital actualization of an individual. In the following pages, we look at different categories of learners in organizations and how to define leadership training and development strategies accordingly.

DIFFERENT CATEGORIES OF
LEARNERS WITHIN ORGANIZATIONS

As stated in the previous chapter, the strength of leadership present within an organization lies not only in the leadership of its upper management, but also in the degree of leadership displayed by the greatest number of employees throughout the firm (Gardner, 1990). As stated by Conger and Pearce (2003), shared leadership occurs at all levels of the organization. Observations of teams in organizations oblige us to recognize that the top visible leaders are "supported by a network of leadership practices distributed throughout the organization" (Fletcher & Käufer, 2003, p. 22).

Even in schools, we need classroom leadership that truly guides, encourages, and enlightens along the way. A new kind of leadership that takes place within the school organization, removed from autocratic style, will engage teachers to develop students' responsibility for their own learning (Lieberman & Miller, 2004).

In order for this leadership to take place at all levels of the organization, we need to recruit and develop individuals who treat their work as an important mission to be accomplished, for themselves and others, and who, in the interest of doing so, are constantly developing their skills (Senge, 1990). But do organizations contain enough of these individuals to provide the strength of collective leadership they need?

Within organizations, there are four categories of learners that can be distributed along the two dimensions of the T learning model: depth and breadth. These four categories of learners, listed below, are shown in figure 3.1:

1. Passive learners
2. Content experts
3. Generalists
4. T learners

Each category corresponds to a different learning attitude, and to different ways in which leadership can be shared throughout the organization. This relationship is explained in the following pages.

Passive Learners

Organizations consist mostly of passive learners. These are individuals whose learning occurs through their day-to day experiences in dealing with their own specific tasks, in direct relation to what is required of them, and through the training programs offered by the organization. Thanks to

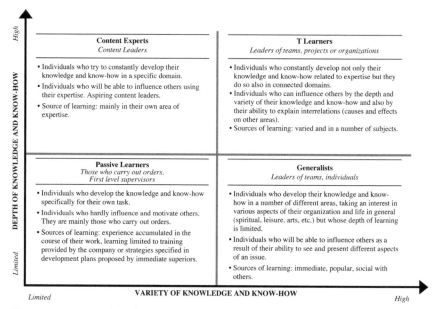

Figure 3.1. Categories of Learners

their years of experience and their knowledge of the organization, these passive learners can become team leaders, supervisors of colleagues, having the ability to help others carry out similar tasks.

This category of learners is represented in the lower left corner of the figure. Their know-how in their own field is gained mainly through experience, and they have a limited understanding of other areas that fall outside their immediate field of responsibility.

These passive learners, if they become team leaders, might have a harder time mobilizing employees to surpass themselves and investing proactively in their own development, due to their own passive learning attitudes.

To increase leadership capacity throughout the organization, training and development programs for this category of employees will be a major contributor. Orientation programs for employees and short assignments in different departments are the most effective methods for providing them with a broader understanding.

Training programs should also allow them to look beyond the narrow confines of their direct working environment and help them to understand the interdependence between their work and other stakeholders such as colleagues, clients, suppliers, shareholders, community. Programs should also give them an overall view of the firm and the industry as a whole. Here are some themes that could be presented during these programs in order to broaden their horizons:

- Organizational perspectives: mission and vision, objectives, strategic objectives, action plan, results and priorities, interdependence between the firm's different functions.
- Client and other stakeholders' perspectives: clients' surveys and feedback, suppliers' needs and issues, community's needs, and so on.
- External environment: best practices, competition overview, threats, future trends and needs.
- Sustainability and the role of ethics in the provision of products and services and the management of resources.
- Any other theme to provide them with a larger perspective.

The more knowledge and know-how this category of learners possesses, the stronger the leadership for the entire organization. In my view, they could also be trained on some basic leadership skills.

Content Experts

The second category of learners is represented in the upper left quadrant of the figure. They are content experts who have mastered a particular area of expertise and, for this reason, are a point of reference for others within the organization. They are less numerous that learners in the previous category.

The organization benefits greatly from the presence of these individuals. They can eventually take on leadership responsibility for an area of activity or an entire team related to their area of expertise. However, their leadership scope is restricted when their expertise dominates exclusively their competence portfolio and they lack a sufficient understanding of related issues. This means that the leadership potential that their expertise gives, while significant, is restricted by a lack of a more global perspective.

The overall organizational leadership is limited when these experts have a limited understanding of the application of their expertise to other subsystems within and outside the organization. In terms of organizational leadership it would be beneficial to introduce these experts to other perspectives through

- Short term assignments within and outside the organization.
- Encounters with other experts or representatives from other departments of the organization.
- Attending conferences related to the organization's industry.
- Complementary training in certain other fields, for example, finances for nonfinancial persons, environment, health, and safety.
- Training in leadership, communication, or management or other complementary aspects.

All these initiatives prove beneficial to the overall level of leadership in the organization by making the limits of their expertise less watertight and by providing broader applications of their intellectual capital throughout the organization or society.

In our knowledge-based modern economy, more and more specialists and experts are emerging. A number of these experts prefer to remain within the limits of their own particular field. Due to the complexity of our organizations, however, it is essential that some of them should also be encouraged to step out of the "comfort zone" that their position as an expert in a given field gives them.

Jean-Francois, an expert on computing and information systems, is a good example. He was equipped with management skills, a certain degree of business sense, strategic thinking, and a sound knowledge of the industry. This is why his superiors offered him a trial opportunity to run a department of the business as they needed someone of his caliber for the position. After a few months, however, Jean-Francois declared openly that he would prefer to stay in his "comfort zone" of computing rather than take on the greater responsibilities that required new learning and new challenges.

The dilemma facing organizations regarding these experts is to develop their leadership within the confines of their own field, while encouraging them to increase the breadth of their knowledge and to take on new responsibilities. However, the complexity with which organizations in today's world operate requires that these experts be encouraged, through various methods, to exercise their leadership both within their own areas of expertise and beyond. Otherwise, organizations become little more than silos of expertise.

Generalists

Those in the third category of learners are generalists. They are represented in the lower right quadrant of the figure. They like to learn about a great number of different fields, but without much depth to any of them. They approach problems from a number of different perspectives. Their main skill and strength is their ability to see and, to a certain extent, understand various aspects of a situation.

Generalists are key members of any team, able to provide different perspectives and bring to light different questions that would otherwise go unnoticed. By doing this, they are already showing a certain level of leadership within their group. These generalists are also, in time, capable of managing multidisciplinary groups or projects, and even a whole organization. They usually surround themselves with genuine experts, but this can represent a risk in certain contexts when the dependency is too high.

A prime example of such a generalist is Arnold. Trained as an accountant, but also interested in many other organizational aspects, he found himself at the head of a manufacturing plant with a few hundred employees. He was at first able to manage well enough when clients were satisfied and targets met. The situation deteriorated when profits fell, engineering problems occurred, and clients became more and more unhappy. The challenge to identify the engineering source of the problem and implement effective operational strategies was too high. He eventually had to resign. External consultants could have helped, but his dependence on their recommendations would have been just as great.

To improve the organization's leadership, decision makers need to make sure that those they recruit for positions involving operational responsibilities first have the same core competencies as the organization itself, whatever these are: education, engineering, transportation, or others. Afterward, training and development strategies, including experiences of all sorts, need to focus on key transversal competencies such as finance, strategic planning, project management, and human resources management. Doing the reverse can represent a serious risk, as the example of Arnold illustrates.

Generalist learners can prove very effective in situations where the ability to mobilize people or the management of a project is more important than a mastery of its specific content. Even in these cases, however, they will still be more effective if they have a grasp of the technical aspects, of the core elements of the central challenge.

T Learners

The fourth and optimal category of learners within an organization is represented in the upper right quadrant of the figure: these are the T learners. These learners have an approach to learning without barriers; they are learners without frontiers. Their T learning attitude is similar in principle to that of boundaryless organizations (Ashkenas, Ulrich, Jick, & Kerr, 2002), which tend to solve their problems by breaking the silos of functions, hierarchies, geography, and specializations and by putting together various individuals who previously dealt exclusively with the aspects of the problem specific to their own field of expertise (marketing, production, customer service, etc.).

T learners develop both depth and transversality, and their cumulative competence and know-how move them beyond the boundaries of a unique specialization. Their leadership capital is therefore optimized and benefits a wider and wider range of situations and people.

This approach to learning allows the extensive actualization of leadership capital by encouraging a better understanding of situations and by providing the individual and the group with a greater degree of influence since in this learning approach lies the comprehension of multiple stakeholders' needs. T learners have the potential to step in when the group is facing situations of greater complexity. A T approach to learning is one that will always be beneficial in both the short and long term to the individuals, teams, and organizations of which they are a part. By encouraging T learning, an organization can increase both the strength and the vitality of its collective leadership and consequently its performance.

DEVELOPING A T LEARNING APPROACH

The complexity of organizations, the speed at which decisions need to be made, the velocity of information, the abundance of control processes, the globalization of challenges, the pressure to balance work and family responsibilities, and many other factors all combine to provide a strong disincentive to taking on the responsibility required by leadership. Consequently, suitable candidates for formal and informal leadership are in short supply (Benimadhu & Gibson, 1999).

Moreover, traditional models of leadership disengage younger generations from their organization. Wishing on the one hand to learn and develop themselves and on the other hand to have a more democratic and participative approach to decisions, they lose motivation rapidly when their environment does not meet their expectations and when traditional models of leadership still prevail. And to top it off, leadership development initiatives are offered to just a few, usually to those in management roles or identified as having high management potential. These individuals usually get all the opportunities, training, and development programs to develop their leadership skills.

A new approach requires developing leadership as a collective resource and not just as an exclusive attribute of just a few, an approach that doesn't impede giving the most challenging leadership roles and opportunities to the most capable ones. It implies, however, developing leadership throughout the whole organization. One way to do that is by encouraging a certain cross-functional learning within organizations. Knowledge about various disciplines can be used to support the collective learning process and assist in discovering cooperatively new ways of solving common problems. Finally, placing T learners in positions of formal leadership can only serve to strengthen the development of a learning approach throughout the organization.

T learning is a key catalyst in leadership actualization, both at the individual and collective levels. A T approach to learning is an essential condition for the development of skills and leadership within organizations. The questions then become, how to identify T learners, how to develop collective T learning within the organization or the community, and to what extent? This is the object of the next section.

How to identify T learners? In today's knowledge-based economy, it is essential that all leaders, managers, team members, and specialists have a strong learning attitude. Those responsible for identifying and developing leadership at any level of an organization would do well to assess management's and teams' learning attitudes in order to develop these further. Various job candidates' learning attitudes and behaviors should also be part of any assessment process.

Here are some examples of a number of elements that should form part of an interview process aimed at identifying the learning attitudes of potential candidates, either from within or outside the organization:

1. What steps have they taken since the beginning of their careers to master different areas of their work? Ask for an example.
2. Can they describe a problem they have dealt with recently, and the steps they took in order to understand all aspects of it? Did they examine all of the elements of this problem, along with its subsystems and their implications? How did they do this?
3. What steps have they taken in order to continue the development of their skills and knowledge?
4. What steps have they taken to develop others?
5. What areas are of interest to them in their professional lives?
6. What sources of information do they use to stay up to date and well informed on areas beyond their immediate area of expertise? Ask for an example.
7. What would they do in order to develop further the skills needed for the specific position being offered?

The following points should also be covered about up-and-coming individuals and potential leadership candidates already within an organization:

- Do they actively keep up to speed with recent developments in their field? Are they familiar with the best practices both within the organization and elsewhere? Are they authorities in their field for the rest of their group? (Content experts)
- Do they tend to be fairly passive as far as the development of their skills is concerned? (Passive learners)
- Do they display the profile of a generalist, trying to understand all the issues related to their field but without much depth? (Generalists)
- Do they have a mastery of one particular area, while also seeking a firm understanding of connected areas? Are they able to deal with multiple

streams of information (clients, suppliers, competitors, discussions with experts, internal and external training, reviews, analysts, etc.) proactively? Do they have the courage to raise questions not directly related to their own area of work whenever necessary? (T learners)
• How open are they to new experiences? What is generally their initial reaction to challenges and changes?
• Can they improve their learning profile? How?

The individuals likely to exercise an optimal form of leadership will tend to be recruited first from among the ranks of T learners and experts, then the generalists. Passive learners can be assigned, at first, more transactional tasks and jobs, but should also benefit from training and development programs providing larger perspectives.

DEVELOPING A COLLECTIVE T LEARNING APPROACH

To what extent shall we focus on the collective development of T learning? The intellectual capital foundation of any organization rests first on the solid expertise related to its core domains of activities. However, the multiplicity of organizational challenges and the multiple areas of expertise within organizations lead all too often to silos of expertise and even a certain retreat of employees behind each one's specific tasks. But solutions and innovations to address clients and community needs can be accomplished only through the sharing of common goals, a common understanding of issues, a common language, and a shared contribution of knowledge and know-how to resolve these. Otherwise, organizations and communities become at risk because of a certain paralysis provoked by specialized perspectives, different priorities, different languages, and different representations of what is needed.

At the collective level, and on top of valuing specialists' expertise and excellence, organizations can develop a collective T learning attitude by

• Having every new employee live the different core jobs within the organization for a certain period of time before they can occupy their official position.

- Encouraging cross-functional teams while making sure the basic terminology of the different fields of expertise is properly understood in order for real dialogue to take place.
- Creating communities of practice where employees can share learning, ideas for resolving common challenges, or thoughts to improve continuously.
- Promoting and encouraging people to take on temporary assignments to local, national, and international projects.
- Sharing best practices within their field of activities.
- Getting specialists out of their comfort zone by assigning them to different projects or jobs, and doing this at different intervals.

Some organizations are more systematic than others in their approach to providing incentives for learning. These firms, such as General Electric, Bombardier, Desjardins Group, Michelin Group, to name but a few, put in place exhaustive formal training and development programs and put much effort into planning the layout for the synergy of teams. At some others, talent management and intellectual capital development is the direct responsibility of the company's president (e.g., GE, Bombardier), and managers are rigorously monitored to ensure that people's development plans are followed.

Development strategies, however, should also take into account which category of learners the different candidates fall into in order to determine their specific needs in terms of training, activities, and the form that their development should take.

So to what extent shall we focus on the collective development of T learning? Group Desjardins, a cooperative banking system, with revenues of over $144 billion and the best return on equity in the financial industry, has answered this question by training thousands of its employees in the T learning approach. According to Jacques Couture, senior director of Desjardins Cooperative Leadership Institute, Desjardins is convinced that it will provide a positive return on their investment. Their leadership program objectives are to improve continuously employees' interdependence, their capacity to work more cooperatively, to innovate and find creative solutions to customers' financial needs. T training aims also at providing true and deep inquiry and reflection.

CONCLUSION

A T learning approach is one of the defining strategies to unleash leadership capacity, at both the individual and the collective levels. T learners and leaders represent an undisputable capacity to transform the "Towers of Babel" that our organizations often become under the restrictive guidance of generalists, or of experts.

And through collective T learning, boundaries slowly disappear, and what emerges is a cocreation leadership process aimed at finding innovative solutions to shared dilemmas and challenges where everyone can contribute, thanks to their expertise and cross-boundary understanding. The scale of this task can seem enormous, but the fact is that T learning can be achieved only gradually by constantly developing our individual and collective knowledge and know-how, one stage at a time, from day one onward.

4

Building Leadership Resilience

If

If you can keep your head when all about you
Are losing theirs and blaming it on you;
If you can trust yourself when all men doubt you,
But make allowance for their doubting too;
If you can wait and not be tired by waiting,
Or, being lied about, don't deal in lies,
Or, being hated, don't give way to hating,
And yet don't look too good, not talk too wise; . . .
Yours is the earth and everything that's in it,
And—which is more—you'll be a Man, my son!

—Rudyard Kipling

Leaders, individuals, and groups, those who have achieved their purpose, have all met with different kinds of adversity at one time or another. Despite all the obstacles in their way, the opposition and threats they have had to face, and the personal and professional rejections they may have suffered, these individuals have continued on in their own chosen direction to achieve their goals. Different popular terms are used to refer to this attitude: perseverance, hard-headedness, engagement or conviction, determination, even passion for the value of their work. All of these are different facets of resilience.

In this chapter, we explore the concept of resilience itself and its importance in the leadership actualization of individuals and teams alike.

Strategies for the development of individual and collective leadership resilience are then presented.

RESILIENCE: DEFINITION AND OVERVIEW

In its original sense, the term resilience refers to the quality of certain materials, with regard to their elasticity and resistance, of resuming their original shape after compression. The term also predates physical science, however. In fact, most religious texts recognize the need for difficult transitions to take place, for periods of obscurity or introspection that allow the attainment of spiritual maturity. Resilience refers to the ability to come through these difficult periods and emerge from them stronger and better adapted than beforehand.

In studies on the subject, resilience is defined as a personal trait, a result, a process, or a skill. Reivich and Shatté (2002) define it as a capacity to overcome past difficulties or traumas, to go through everyday adversities, to bounce back from a major setback or life-altering event. Moen and Erickson (1995) define it as "the capacity to cope with life setbacks and challenges" (p. 175), while Rutter (1999) describes resilience as a term "used to describe relative resistance to psychosocial risk experiences" (p. 119).

We define it as the ability and process taking place when someone is facing obstacles and problems, meeting adversity head on and overcoming it, recovering from setbacks and failures, and accepting life's challenges with confidence and perseverance. The study of resilience brings together elements of neuropsychology, genetics, psychology, and psychobiology, making it a complex subject. According to Cyrulnik (2003) the study of resilience restores a degree of hope by highlighting our ability to overcome difficulties and be content.

Resilience Development in Children

Psychological researchers, and those in other associated disciplines, have taken a close interest in the resilience present among some children coming from difficult or troubled backgrounds (Brooks & Goldstein, 2003; Clarke & Clarke, 2003; Rutter, 1999; Werner & Smith, 1989). These researchers spent a number of years charting the progress of children from areas in which drug addiction, poverty, and crime were rife. Their goal in doing so was to identify the attitudes, strategies, and qualities shared by those who succeeded in overcoming these problems and went on to lead relatively normal, well-adjusted adult lives.

Although resilience is the product of a number of different and multiple factors (personal, interpersonal, and environmental), the authors conclude that resilience is developed through certain specific strategies (Werner & Smith, 1992). In order for people to overcome their difficult childhood,

1. They succeed in establishing and maintaining relationships that are good for them, for example, with a neighbor, a teacher, or a relative. They have a positive social orientation.
2. They adopt a proactive attitude toward difficult or delicate situations, rather than remaining passive. They have self-help skills.
3. They are full of curiosity. They observe, ask questions, and search for answers. They demonstrate alertness.
4. They tend to distance themselves from their dysfunctional families, recognizing that the dysfunctions belong to their parents and siblings rather than to themselves.

In the wake of this research, more and more programs aiming at developing resilience are being offered in schools, particularly in the United States.

Leadership and Resilience

Although a great deal of the research into resilience is based on the observation of children from difficult backgrounds (abusive parents, violent or crime-ravaged areas, war zones), my own observations and interviews with leaders have highlighted the importance of this capacity or process for unleashing leadership potential, since leadership involves taking risks, facing oppositions, frustrations, or setbacks.

Moreover, it also appears that unleashing and exercising leadership also build resilience, through the learning that takes places, and the process of building self-efficacy that it involves. This is valid both for individuals and for groups. In order for an individual to accomplish a vision or a purpose, to implement change, and to overcome adversity, resilience must be part of the game. The strategies that these leaders have taken to face adversity are presented in the following pages and synthesized in a resilience development model.

Examples abound in our representations of great leaders who have encountered great opposition: Gandhi, who fought for Indians' rights in South Africa, then in India, even tough laws at the time and British power were strong opposing forces; Churchill, who fought Hitler despite, at the beginning, the parliament's lukewarm support, a not-so-well-equipped British army, and a totalitarian regime armed to the teeth; Rosa Parks, who faced the adversity of the white bus driver and then the police without giving up her right to sit where she was.

On a smaller scale, the same is true of all those who dedicate themselves wholeheartedly to their professional or organizational lives and goals. Adversity is a fact of life for all those who feel they have a contribution to make, a specific path to follow, or who just want to realize their purpose.

Leadership and Collective Resilience

On top of their own resilience, leaders also build collective resilience of teams, classrooms, organizations, and communities through their behaviors and attitudes, but also by words that encourage others and give them hope, pride, and trust in themselves. This is what Churchill expressed in many of his actions such as visits on battlefields and speeches like this one to the House of Commons when England was realizing her lonesome fight against the German troops: "Let us therefore brace ourselves to our duties, and so bear ourselves that if the British Empire and its Commonwealth last for a thousand years, men will still say, 'This was their finest hour'" (Churchill, 2003 [June 18, 1940]).

Adversity increases in proportion to the extent of the exercise of leadership that is required. As Pliny the Younger (an ancient historian) once said, "Prosperity tries the fortunate, adversity the great." Adversity proves useful in the development of leadership. When used as a learning tool, it can strengthen us by

- Increasing our familiarity with facing various forms and degrees of adversity.

- Building our confidence in our ability to face any problems we may encounter.
- Developing leadership skills such as defending a point of view, negotiating, managing difficult situations, or reaching a consensus in difficult situations while maintaining a positive perspective.
- Allowing us to see other unforeseen, important points of view thanks to opposition or resistance to our ideas and projects.

Therefore, we have everything to gain from facing adversity and developing our resilience in order not only to unleash leadership capital but also to strengthen it. Before presenting strategies to build leadership resilience, here is first a description of different forms of adversity.

THE DIFFERENT FORMS OF ADVERSITY

There are three main categories of adversity that we might face, learn to manage, and build on in order to further capitalize our leadership:

1. External adversity, from either situations or people.
2. Internal adversity, coming from our self-imposed boundaries, our beliefs, and our internal discourse.
3. The general culture of comfort seeking and materialism in our societies.

Each category of adversity is described in the following pages. Table 4.1 provides an overview of the different forms of adversity.

External Adversity

External adversity is composed of the various forms of opposition, difficulties, and challenges present in the individual's environment. This adversity can be subtle or more direct, even hostile. It can manifest itself as a lack of support from those around us, exclusion from various groups, united opposition or coalition, indirect boycotting, personal defeats and failures, or even direct and aggressive attacks.

Table 4.1.   Different Forms of Adversity

External Adversity	*Internal Adversity*	*Material Comfort*
• Lack of support from friends and peers • Lack or loss of trust by superiors or team members • Exclusion from groups • United opposition or coalitions • Rumors and other indirect forms of boycotting • Harassment • Direct, aggressive attacks • Personal failures and defeats, dismissals	• Poor self-understanding of our talents, interests • Not learning from previous experiences • Self-criticism • Imposing false limits or boundaries (e.g., age, education), fear of risks, perfectionism • Lack of life purpose or projects • Lack of personal vision	• Easily attainable material comfort • Values and social pressures of our in-groups • Access to revenue streams not of our own making • Undemanding nature of parents, teachers, superiors, or colleagues • Easy access to numerous forms of entertainment • Constant distractions

Being dismissed or being denied a project, a job, or a promotion are other forms of adversity. These setbacks can increase our vulnerability if we give in to them, causing us to feel discouraged, doubt ourselves, and question our professional value, and affecting our view of ourselves as being useful to society as well as losing a certain amount of social recognition. These situations can be even more traumatizing when they arise unexpectedly creating more stress.

Other different manifestations of external adversity are being left out of the decision-making process for any reason, whether as the result of a difference of opinion, ideas, interests, affinities, or status; a refusal on the part of colleagues to collaborate and share knowledge or know-how; and even vicious rumors. Jean-Pierre paid the price for one of these manifestations when, despite having the abilities needed to be a team leader, one or two opponents spread false rumors about his teamwork performance so that he wouldn't be offered a promotion involving team responsibilities and duties.

Of all the forms of external adversity, direct attacks are those feared by most people, often because of the aggressive nature of these attacks on our ideas, our projects or, worse still, on us personally. They can affect our sense of self-worth since they tend to create a sense of rejection. Philippe went through such an ordeal. He was a young prospective leader in a growing business, but was berated by his direct supervisor in front of his colleagues for a recent poor performance. Aggressive, direct attacks like this one can be very harmful to individuals' self-esteem and to their confidence within the group. To exercise leadership, we need to manage these forms of external adversity as there will always be occasions when, justly or unjustly, we might have to face them.

Internal Adversity

A completely different but nevertheless major form of adversity results from the limitations we impose on ourselves. Adversity of this type is perhaps the most difficult for prospective leaders to overcome, as it is the most underestimated, the most subtle, the most silent yet pervasive one and, therefore, capable of causing the most damage. Without in any way undermining the importance of overcoming the other forms of adversity, it is absolutely essential that we confront and overcome our own internal adversity in order to actualize our leadership capital.

This "inner enemy" can take a number of different forms:

- Self-criticism
- Imposing false limitations on ourselves
- Insufficient knowledge of ourselves
- Perfectionism
- Lack of personal vision

A form of internal adversity that can harm leadership capital development is self-criticism. Early in her career, Anne Lauvergeon (the CEO of AREVA, recognized as one of the world's most powerful business women) confided to me (June 21, 2001) that she had a habit of criticizing herself too often and too harshly, never really feeling capable of handling the challenges that faced her. At an early stage, however, she realized that this habit of self-criticism was blocking the very energy she needed to face and overcome outer challenges, learn, and do her job. She decided to stop it, focusing instead on her tasks.

Criticism is particularly harmful when we attribute failure or difficulties to a lack of aptitudes (such as intelligence). This form of self-criticism reduces self-efficacy or our beliefs in our own ability to succeed. Thereafter, this weakened self-efficacy considerably affects the performance and the amount of effort we invest in succeeding (Bandura, 1997).

In his professional life, Henry used to shy away from putting himself or his ideas forward due to his fear of being ridiculed or becoming the object of derision and criticism. He had internalized his father's criticisms, who regularly told his son that he couldn't succeed, that his ideas weren't as good as others', and that it was better for him to keep a low profile. He gradually learned to trust himself and his own capacities through experience and support, and more specifically when another authority figure gave him greater responsibilities while assuring him of his support.

Often, our past relationships with family members, parents as well as siblings, can explain the restraints we place on ourselves in actualizing our leadership capital, our parents providing us with our first model of leadership. They are our first supporters, and our siblings are our first allies or followers. While it can help explain our internal dialogue, it does not determine forever how we shall treat ourselves.

Francis systematically rejected anything he associated with his father. This counterdependence or systematic opposition held him back from knowing and accessing his own true talents and interests until the day he finally discovered that he shared with his father the same financial talent but not necessarily the same values. It was only through self-knowledge that he was finally able to understand and accept the fact that he actually had an aptitude for and an interest in finance, just like his father. By understanding better who we are, what it is that we like and dislike, we can give ourselves the freedom to work toward our own interests and values.

The restrictions that individuals place on themselves can also stem from the fear of taking risks, which manifests itself in many ways: perfectionism, fear of making mistakes, fear of criticism, a low tolerance for unknown or ambiguous situations, and fear of losing what we already have, such as comfort, emotional bonds, and recognition within our current groups. This fear of taking risks, however, has the effect of limiting the energy and the potential that we have and our capacity to capitalize on any important opportunities that may come our way. It is up to each of us to decide how much risk to take at any given moment. However, when this apprehension is running our lives, it must be confronted as if it were an enemy invading our home.

Since the fear of taking risks decidedly does not enable leadership, it is essential that it be tamed and mastered in order for leadership capital to be actualized. It is therefore necessary first to identify our fears and then to neutralize them one by one. This can be done alone, or with the help of trainers, coaches, or mentors.

Lacking a personal vision of what we want to accomplish or become is a fourth source of internal adversity, as it restricts us in committing ourselves and investing our time and energy in something we really value. People who have not yet taken the time to clarify their personal vision or objectives can only invest themselves in short-term activities or be lukewarm followers of others' purposes. On the other hand, people who have a clear vision, who imagine a better future, work toward its realization, mobilizing themselves and others along the way.

External and internal adversities are the most recognized inhibitors of leadership actualization. But there is a third and underestimated one, which is the culture of comfort and materialism as an end in itself.

The Culture of Comfort Seeking and Materialism

Excessive exposure to adversity can, in some cases, prove harmful to individuals' leadership capital. However, a lack of adversity can prove just as harmful. In fact, facing too few challenges or difficulties can itself present a major obstacle to actualizing leadership capital and leading a meaningful life.

The pursuit of comfort and personal well-being has become increasingly important for many people in our contemporary society. However, this love of comfort seriously inhibits the growth and development of leadership and leaders. Difficult, stressful, or challenging situations are then viewed with apprehension rather than as opportunities for personal growth. This pursuit of comfort comes from a number of different sources, namely

- Lack of expectations from authority figures such as parents, teachers, managers, and employers as well as from ourselves.
- The pressures and values of our in-groups, as well as media reinforcement of the materialistic symbols of happiness.

- The availability of many and varied forms of entertainment with which to distract ourselves from our true aspirations and potential.
- The ease of attaining material comfort.
- The opportunity to benefit from sources of income that are not of our own making (inheritance, rent, government or spouse assistance).

DEVELOPING RESILIENCE

How can we develop resilience in order to enhance our leadership capital? How have leaders learned to face and overcome adversity of all sorts? How did these individuals become so resilient? What development strategies did they use? How can we develop resilience in others? The answers to these questions are presented in this section.

The actualization of leadership capital requires the development of a certain amount of courage in the face of adversity, coupled with the ability to find a constructive response to the problems we are faced with. It is a necessary capacity whether for family, school, community, or work. Parents, teachers, and school principals, citizens and politicians, employees and managers, we all need it to further unleash our leadership capital. This ability is one that develops gradually and continuously. Just as for maintaining and improving health, however, it too requires constant effort in order to grow.

In the following pages, a model for the development of resilience to allow the actualization of leadership capital is presented. It addresses the various different forms of adversity that can arise.

A Conceptual Model for Developing Resilience

The main strategies for developing resilience are grouped along four main axes, as shown in figure 4.1. These strategies are on top of healthy habits and stress-management efforts. These four axes are

1. Personal
2. Interpersonal
3. Professional
4. Social or collective

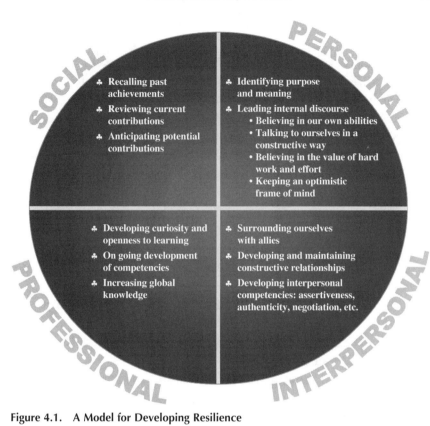

Figure 4.1. A Model for Developing Resilience

The Personal Dimension

The foundations of the ability to overcome adversity and actualize leadership capital are first internal—that is to say, they are closely linked to the ability to clarify our goals, aspirations, personal values, and beliefs while maintaining a constructive internal discourse.

Victor Frankl (1984), a psychiatrist and Auschwitz survivor, observed that his companions in the concentration camp, in order to survive, had to find a reason to continue living and thus a meaning in their suffering. He observed that those with a specific goal to live for, such as a fiancé, a sibling, a friend, a project back home, an objective for the day, had more inner strength than the other prisoners. They also had a greater chance of surviving. Conversely, those who had lost all meaning in their lives became depressed and rapidly fell ill. He even established a method of identifying prisoners at risk in order to prevent them from falling prey to depression.

Frankl, therefore, made it his goal to help others understand the inhuman experience of the concentration camps. He looked toward the future, picturing himself giving speeches on the psychology of the concentration camps to rapt conference audiences. He went on to create a form of therapy based on meaning and rationality known as logotherapy. According to this psychiatrist, human beings' search for the meaning of their lives is one of the basic driving forces of life. Frankl highlights Nietzsche's observation: "He who has a why to live can bear almost any how" (pp. 97, 101).

It is up to every individual to carry out this search—no one else can do it for us. We are responsible for asking ourselves the big question, then finding our own answers. These answers can evolve over the years as the nature of our lives changes.

When an individual doesn't have a clear goal in life, he becomes more vulnerable to the changes taking place around him: staff cuts, economic crises, other unexpected events. On the other hand, having a clear goal in life strengthens resilience.

Enhancing leadership requires a goal to pursue, and this goal becomes a resilience tool builder. To begin with, leaders' goals are often fairly vague, and then become clearer as time goes on. For example, Maria Fernandez—the immigrant and successful entrepreneur—told herself from an early age that she would do everything in her power to become a respected individual, even if the specific parameters of this respect were as yet undefined (personal communications, May 17, 2000, and June 2001). Her goal was vague at first but got more precise as time went by.

Louis, the CEO of an international business, wanted to be a responsible person capable of creating an environment in which individuals could grow in confidence while also satisfying their families' needs. He wanted to be the complete opposite of his father, who abandoned his wife and their five young children.

Life goals change and develop, and their value cannot be judged by anyone but the individuals they belong to. For, as Frankl (1984) states, "These tasks, and therefore the meaning of life, differ from man to man and from moment to moment" (p. 98). These life goals help to provide individuals with direction, a real raison d'être, a source of motivation.

They also help with the decision-making process when opportunities present themselves and in finding a fighting spirit in the face of obstacles or difficulties, as long as they are strong and firmly rooted in the individual's deepest desires.

So before going on with the next set of strategies, take the time to reflect on these questions:

- What do you want to accomplish in your life, in the following years or even this year?
- What is your purpose, your goal?
- Leading your life means what to you? What is important for you?
- Who is important to you?
- What do you envision for your group (family, team, organization) in the years to come: in 2, 3, or 10 years?

Another strategy for developing leadership resilience requires us to be aware of our internal discourse and to lead it. Gaining awareness of our internal discourse and of its negative elements in particular is, therefore, an essential step if we wish to increase the energy and determination at our disposal when facing challenges. It involves reviewing our own belief system and thoroughly scrutinizing our internal discourse regarding

- Ourselves. The first and most frequent relationship we have is with ourselves, therefore the need to be talking to ourselves in positive and constructive terms.
- Our leadership abilities. Examine how you view leadership and your own capacity. Do you see it as something you can improve or something permanent, determined by uncontrollable factors? To view leadership development as your unique responsibility unleashes tremendous energy, unimagined.
- The level of effort needed to succeed. For example, if effort seems too important in regard to your purpose, break the overall task into smaller steps and address each one, step by step.
- The reasons used to explain our successes and failures. Any project or purpose is doomed to face difficulties at any given time. Failures or rejections call for more efforts or different strategies in order for you to succeed.

- How we see our present and future. Optimistic people, and those who have a positive view of their capacity, tend to expend much effort in pursuing their goal and get closer to its realization (Bandura, 1997). You can reprogram your views about your present and future, but the first step starts with being aware of these.

The use of a notebook or a journal is a good starting tool to become aware of our internal thoughts. Once we are aware of these, then the use of the following strategies is most helpful:

1. Talking to yourself in a positive or constructive way. Stop and remove depreciating thoughts; transform these right away in positive terms such as "I can; I am progressing; I am getting better at . . ."
2. Believing in the value of hard work and effort. Get into the habit of telling yourself that popular adage, "Practice makes perfect."
3. Keeping an optimistic frame of mind. Recall, for example, who your supporters, your allies are; what your past achievements are, and who will benefit from your work.
4. Taking on leadership experiences of progressive difficulty. To become resilient at exercising leadership roles or actions, challenge yourself by getting out of your comfort zone, but do this at a feasible difficulty level. Equip yourself with a learning will, reflection time on your learning, and key allies.

The first set of the above strategies involves being your best friend, a friend to whom you talk nicely, whom you encourage, give positive and constructive feedback, and certainly not a friend who criticizes or downplays you. Being your best friend means that you congratulate yourself when you succeed or make progress. It means that you tell yourself that your efforts to achieve something are worth it and that you will succeed as long as you give to it the necessary effort. And if you fail, tell yourself that at least you have tried, and you have learned something from it that will be useful next time around. Finally, as your best friend would do, highlight your qualities and leadership skills.

Leaders and resilient people take the credit that is associated with their successes, small ones as well as bigger ones. They may also recognize their team's effort and know-how, but they nevertheless emphasize that accomplishments happen by virtue of their direct involvement and input. This attitude of attributing success, progress, small and bigger victories to our efforts and contribution build determination.

The second set of strategies involves believing in the value of hard work and effort. Recall a success that you have accomplished in your life, at home, at school, at work or in the community. How do you explain it? Make sure you attribute it to your direct input. Getting into the discipline of reframing your explanations by telling yourself that success or progress is due to the work and effort you put into it and to your own competence. Sure, sometimes success happens because of pure luck, but be aware that constant attribution to external factors is detrimental to a sense of personal efficacy and resilience.

A third set of strategies has to do with a discipline of maintaining an optimistic yet realistic outlook toward a better future for yourselves and the groups you are part of. Optimism brings hope, which is an essential component of resilience (when combined with strong self-belief and a strong conviction in the value of hard work and effort). Optimism mainly stems from the manner in which we analyze and discuss things, both internally and with other people. Therefore, a discussion tainted by a defeatist outlook or placing a disproportionate emphasis on negative or uncontrollable factors will clearly damage your ability to motivate yourself as well as those around you. As stated by de Vries (2001), showing leadership also means bringing hope to others.

So avoid self-talk or sentences such as these: "It won't work"; "I am or we are going to fail"; "There is nothing we can do about it." Instead, get into the habit of using self-talk and phrases similar to the following ones: "I am worth it"; "it is possible"; "I have all it takes"; "I am doing what is required to succeed"; "I am surrounded with good friends and allies."

The fourth category of personal strategies to develop leadership resilience is taking on leadership experiences of progressive difficulty and therefore building on these experiences to reinforce beliefs in your ability to succeed. As Eleanor Roosevelt wrote in her autobiography, "Every time you meet a situation, though you think at the time it is an impossibility, and you go through the torture of the damned, once you have met it and lived through it, you find that forever after you are freer than you were before" (Roosevelt, 1960, p. 29).

Combined with other strategies described above and below, leadership experiences will not only strengthen your leadership self-efficacy beliefs, but they will develop your capacity to face adversity and persevere despite it. So, look around your neighborhood, your school, your community, your organization. Are there any leadership behaviors, tasks, or experiences that you could undertake?

Cutting out pointless and harmful self-criticism, being our best friend, making the necessary effort to succeed, taking up challenges on top of visualizing ourselves succeeding, carrying out constructively assessments of our performance, learning from the mistakes made along the way and laughing at ourselves when necessary—all of these are strong driving forces of resilience, a key ingredient of leadership actualization. Our resilience and self-leadership also create an energy that we transmit to those around us. This energy is a key factor in mobilizing others.

The Interpersonal Dimension

The interpersonal dimension of the resilience development model is concerned with the relationships we choose and establish with those around us. Surrounding ourselves with people who are able to accompany or support us on our journey of personal development is key to leadership self-actualization.

In 1955, Emily Werner, from the University of California, began a study of the lives of various children coming from difficult or abusive backgrounds. This study lasted more than 30 years, and revealed that one of the most important abilities possessed by those who succeeded despite their difficult starting point was that of establishing at least one important relationship with someone outside their immediate family circle such as a grandparent, a teacher, or a neighbor (Werner & Smith, 1989, 1992).

Realizing that they were different and stronger than their unfortunate parents, the more resilient children sought out individuals who provided them with the care, affection, and support that they needed. Their ability to make use of this external support was essential, as it provided them with a social framework. Individuals—children in particular—who establish these new social and emotional bonds are better equipped to face any problems or traumas they may encounter in the course of their lives.

More so than the quantity, it is the quality of some key relationships that has a bearing on the amount of leadership actualization and resilience these bring about, not only during the early years of a career but over the course of our entire lives. Dynamic energy, an important quality in any leader and one essential to the act of leadership itself, has many sources, but one of these is undoubtedly the ability to form relationships with people who strengthen our confidence, willpower, and goals. Therefore, what relationships are the most meaningful to you and what do you do to nurture these relationships?

The Professional Dimension

The professional dimension of the model is defined as the overall competence we gradually build outside the home involvement. It generally involves work but also includes volunteer work or political or community services. In itself, professional competence is a lever both to resilience and to leadership actualization by permitting us to grow our self-confidence, our sense of purpose, our contribution potential and to be recognized by our groups. We can rely on our competence when faced with challenges and adversity. The depth and breadth of skills possessed by an individual reduces his or her sense of vulnerability when economic difficulties arise. Those clearly in possession of important knowledge or know-how have a greater chance of finding other alternatives.

Resilience in adapting to change, on the other hand, is increased when the individual has a wealth of knowledge and know-how. Openness to organizational or technological change is most often found in those who expand continuously their professional abilities and personal competencies.

The ongoing development of skills has also been shown to be an excellent agent of resilience development, allowing the individual to be less vulnerable to the effects of changes such as staffing cutbacks and economic crises. Moreover, skilled individuals, or those who constantly develop their abilities, have more chance of being retained by a company or of finding a new position elsewhere—either in the same industry or in another field altogether.

Knowledge and know-how, acting as catalysts to the development of resilience, imply by their presence a certain degree of openness to learning. Curiosity, or openness to learning, is linked to the development of resilience in children (Killian, 2004), but also in adults as it requires us to learn about the different aspects of a situation or problem. The difficulties present in a challenging situation then are seen as opportunities for the individual to learn. The motivation to learn or display curiosity can also be triggered when an individual feels he or she has a deficit in a particular area.

It was this openness to learning, in part, that saved Frankl (1984) during his time in the concentration camp. He adopted an inquisitive, learning attitude in response to the extreme adversity he was faced with so that, in years to come, he would be able to pass on to others what he had learned. Moreover, curiosity and appetite for learning give meaning to difficulties encountered on top of providing a means of protection and a kind of objectivity.

One final element of professional know-how, as a basis for resilience, is global knowledge, defined as the extended understanding of our environment, be it through knowledge of history, a general understanding of the dynamics of individuals, organizations, industries, peoples, or cultures, or through knowledge of different strategies and styles of communication. This global knowledge means that, in addition to having a broader view of any given situation, we can also put problems into perspective, find solutions, and provide a response inspired by this broader awareness. Individuals possessing this global knowledge are also equipped with a greater number of strategies for communication and negotiation, which are key leadership skills.

Being interculturally competent gives us access to a greater range of communication strategies, as every culture has its own approach to communication and problem solving. Moreover, having more knowledge and better communication skills increases our ability to influence a wider range of situations, in addition to increasing our confidence in our own ability to succeed.

Nothing guarantees total resilience in the face of any possible difficulty, but some strategies, such as continuous professional development, curiosity, and openness to learning, are certainly most beneficial. And as stated by the GLOBE researchers group (House et al., 2002), task competence (e.g., administratively competent, being informed, excellence, or performance orientation) is a universal attribute valued in the 130 cultures participating in their study. So, what do you do to continuously develop your competence?

The Social Dimension

The social dimension of the resilience development model consists of our present and potential contribution to another person or to a given group, be it a classroom, a team, an organization, or even a group of parents, citizens, or clients. The main benefit of contributing to the well-being of another individual or group, besides the results, is that it allows us to take the focus off ourselves, our problems, and our various opponents and instead concentrate on the needs of others.

All of our collective achievements—past and present—reinforce our beliefs in our own ability to get things done, to be of use to others, and to be able to do so again in the future. Past achievements can be recalled in difficult moments and times of adversity. Expected achievements, those that we believe possible despite adversity, are equally important as they provide us and our groups (teams, families) with a motivational vision and a goal for the future.

Among the leaders studied, many have developed a strong belief over the course of their careers in their ability to contribute something of value to their group, based on their record of previous achievements. This firm conviction in their contribution gives them strength at difficult times in their lives, such as when dealing with setbacks, failures, or major obstacles.

Cécile Bonnefond, the current president of Veuve Clicquot Ponsardin, showed this kind of conviction in her self-worth while foreseeing the sudden closure of a French division of Nestlé, of which she was the director (personal communication, June 22, 2000). This strength of conviction allowed her to face and overcome the problem when it finally happened.

A converse example is one of a school principal that I met who doesn't see the same potential for his contribution if he were to be dismissed from his current role. This blockage provokes in him a sense of panic that further diminishes his capacity to overcome the current adversity. He gets more and more tense, frustrated, resentful, and even vengeful when facing his current opponents.

Social contributions—past, present, and future—represent another of the fundamental building blocks of resilience. For your own benefit, list your social or collective contributions: those you have made, those that you are currently involved in, and maybe some future potential ones. You can even draw a second list, one directly related to contributions made when exercising leadership roles or behaviors. Preserve these lists and come back to them during harsh times.

Developing Leadership and Collective Resilience

Teams of all kinds now provide the driving force for all types of organizations: community, schools, or business organizations. You can even consider your own family as a team. On top of developing your own leadership resilience, you might also want to develop the collective leadership resilience of groups that are important to you. Consequently, this section exposes strategies to develop collective leadership resilience, which is the resilience of groups to demonstrate leadership, to continue in their struggles in spite of oppositions, adversity, and other difficulties. Collective resilience is an important factor in the actualization and practice of shared leadership.

The development of teams' collective resilience occurs similarly to the way it does at the individual level. Collective leadership resilience can be strengthened by

1. A motivational and shared vision of the future to accomplish together and that allows the team to put their problems in perspective and understand the goal at which all their efforts are directed. This shared vision follows shared understanding of key issues. As stated by Coutu (2002), "Staring down reality, though grueling, enables organizations to train themselves to survive before the fact" (p. 46).
2. A positive, constructive, optimistic (but not naïve), energetic dialogue between the group's members. The quality of the dialogue is key to collective resilience. Recall the impact of constructive self-talk, and value the same quality between and about team members.
3. The conviction, shared by every member of the group, that they have the ability to succeed. For this, first and if possible, pay attention to the group composition, then make sure that the competencies of every member and the whole group are known and recognized. Recall past accomplishments and the effort required to succeed. Then make

sure that the group shares common beliefs regarding their aggregate capabilities, as these beliefs provide the needed protection against discouragement (Bandura, 1997). To top it off, give the group autonomy and control over the strategies to achieve their goals.

4. Emphasizing the importance of effort and perseverance. Beliefs in the importance of hard work and effort clearly act as catalysts of leadership actualization. Collective resilience can be developed by prizing excellence and perseverance in the face of challenges. Coaches, trainers, and mentors encourage resilience development and leadership actualization when focusing on these values and attitudes.

5. Developing interpersonal and teamworking skills by making sure that group members continuously work better together. This can be done through training but also by providing shared moments to reflect upon successes, setbacks, and lessons learned.

6. Value openness to learning in addition to the collective competence. Ask questions that assist group members to reflect upon their learning and to reveal unseen perspectives.

7. Providing progressive experiences to allow challenges as well as potential for success.

Resilience, be it for individuals or collectives, is not an everlasting acquired characteristic. It needs to be revisited regularly in order for people to maintain and reinforce it, if only because life changes and with it, the nature of adversity.

CONCLUSION

Being resilient means facing difficult situations and emerging from the experience a stronger person than we were before, even when the experience has been traumatic in some way. It is the ability to live, develop, and succeed despite adversity.

Organizations and groups, in whatever form, benefit greatly from the presence of individuals and teams displaying individual and collective resilience. These benefits are accrued both in terms of the quality of the working environment and in productivity gains; resilient people are clearly more confident, dynamic, perseverant motivators and sources of inspiration.

The development of resilience is both a condition and a consequence of the actualization and exercising of leadership in difficult and demanding situations. With resilience, recognized as one of the essential elements of leadership (Bennis & Thomas, 2002), it is clear that developing this capacity among young professionals and potential leadership candidates is a key ingredient of leadership. An increasing number of leadership development programs now include activities aimed at the development of resilience.

5

Seeking Leadership Developers

During their path to leadership actualization, leaders have encountered different individuals who, implicitly or explicitly, influenced them and acted as mentors, coaches, passeurs (people who connect individuals together or pass on valuable information), challengers, role models, or even anti-models. The impact that these actors had on the leaders studied allowed them to strengthen the foundations of their leadership capital, even at times when they still had no idea of what they wanted to become. This chapter describes six key developer roles that actualize leadership capital.

LEADERSHIP DEVELOPERS

Many examples abound of leaders who, thanks to meaningful relationships and dramatic encounters, started on a path that would change their views of themselves and of their lives forever. This is the case of Martine Clement (personal communication, May 2, 2000), one leader and entrepreneur I met in France. With the help of a high school teacher, she spent a year living in Portland, Maine, United States, as part of an exchange program with an American family. This decision became a turning point; her American host parents turned out to be strong leadership models for her: the mother was a community leader, while the father was a Harvard professor.

Following this experience, Martine came home stronger, able to overcome many barriers, studying chemical engineering, in a traditionally male-dominated university program at a time when it was still the exception for a woman to obtain a degree in this field. She then became more and more involved in the family business, even contrary to her father's wishes.

Martine was influenced by a number of different people in her leadership development, and each of these played a different yet important role. The first of them, besides her father, were her high school teacher, who provided her with life-changing information; the mother of the American family, who demonstrated the importance of contributing to the improvement of a community as a whole; the American father, who insisted on the importance of a scientific outlook and thorough reasoning in addressing problems; a consultant who acted as her coach; and a Jesuit who provided her with guidance regarding the often troublesome task of managing her life and the business. Another close adult acted as an anti-model of leadership because of her adamant pessimism, lack of initiative, and sensitivity to social pressure of all kinds.

We all encounter many important or meaningful individuals in the course of our lives, but they can contribute to our development only if we acknowledge them, listen to them, and develop significant relationships with them whenever possible. This ability to create positive relationships is also one of the strategies adopted by children born into difficult environments who manage to defy the odds and grow out of them through nurturing their positive relationship with a teacher, a neighbor, or a grandparent (Clarke & Clarke, 2003). This ability to form relationships with significant individuals and benefit from their experience and teachings is also crucial to the actualization of leadership capital.

The different roles that these significant individuals can play are presented in the following pages. Learning to recognize these roles is essential to progress more rapidly to your next level of leadership development. And anyone who can play one of these roles is better equipped to do so when these roles are better understood and the impact better directed. The impact of the input might take effect at a later development stage, without you being ever aware of it.

Throughout the years, interviews with leaders and my experience in leadership development have allowed me to identify six main roles that can be played by key individuals in their relationships with others on their path to leadership actualization:

1. Mentors
2. Coaches
3. Challengers
4. Passeurs
5. Role models
6. Anti-models

These leadership developers take different actions with their apprentices of leadership: directing or orienting, teaching, challenging, putting apprentices in contact with other key individuals, or providing inspiration by giving either a positive example or even a negative one. More precisely:

- A mentor orients by the reflective questions asked and through reflections on the meaning of our experiences, our work, or our commitment.
- The coach instructs, allowing us to gain specific new skills and knowledge.
- The challenger provides us with high expectations and demanding opportunities, and invites us to overcome them and surpass ourselves.
- The passeur puts us in contact with other individuals who might have an important impact on us or show us a different view of the world, or gives us life-changing information.
- The role model inspires us with the values, behaviors, and achievements displayed.
- As far as the anti-model is concerned, the strength of the negative example provided inspires us to do better.

Figure 5.1 illustrates the different ways in which these different actors can influence us in unleashing leadership capital. A more complete description of each role is provided below.

The Mentor

The origin of the term mentor is usually attributed to Homer's *Odyssey*, in which Mentor is the loyal friend and advisor of Telemachus and

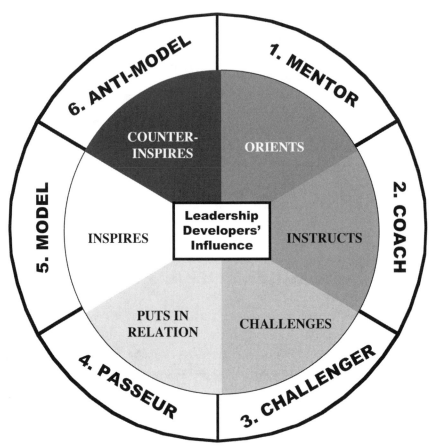

Figure 5.1. Influence of Leadership Developers

teaches him how to act as king while Ulysses is absent (Little, Fowler, & Coulson, 1955). However, some authors (Roberts, 1999) dispute this origin, and even question the mentoring role of Mentor: "But, was the original Mentor wisdom incarnate? Did he guide, counsel, advise, and enable the young Telemachus?" (para. 12). In a subsequent article on the subject, Roberts (2000), following a phenomenological literature review of mentoring, found that the concept is referred to in the literature as having eight essential attributes: a process, a form, a relationship, a helping process, a teaching-learning process, a reflective practice, a career and personal development process, and a formalized process and a role constructed by or for a mentor.

In a leadership development role and in my own view, a mentor is a person who guides and directs us in the clarification and establishment of our values, our personal vision, and our private, professional, or organizational goals. Mentors bring with them a degree of wisdom or experience that allows us to develop a long-term view through the questions, reflections, and advice they provide. Mentors maintain a longer term perspective than those exercising a coaching role. A mentor is especially helpful during difficult existential periods when we are questioning ourselves or experiencing changes in our life.

By asking the right questions mentors help us to think by ourselves without actually providing us with answers. They support us by encouraging introspection through their comments, personal observations, experience, and maturity.

Good mentoring allows aspiring leaders to further develop their own powers of reflection and analysis, their intellectual, scientific, and moral strength. The impact of mentoring is most significant when the values mentors pass on through their questions and reflections are ethical, strong on social responsibility and the sustainable development of individuals and organizations, when they support without controlling or manipulating their protégés on their unique journey, allowing them to become progressively independent.

Sulkowicz (2004), a psychoanalyst and a top consultant to management teams, alerts CEOs to the potential dangers that mentors, or close confidants, may sometimes represent: "But unless leaders examine their own motives, and those of their confidants, these relationships will almost certainly be dangerous, and sometimes even catastrophic" (p. 65).

Mentors can be internal or external to an organization. Mentoring programs within organizations provide their protégés with

- Debriefing sessions to discuss learning experiences and challenges, hoping to consolidate and shorten mentorees' learning curve.
- Assistance in discussing career paths and choices within the organization.
- Orientation, instilling them with the organization's values and culture.

Difficulties arise with mentoring programs when there is a lack of continuity in the established relationships for various reasons such as conflicting priorities or a lack of real commitment to the mentoring program on the part of the individual or the organization. It also happens that formal mentoring programs fail to run their full course due to a lack of compatibility between the mentor and his or her protégé. For an effective mentoring experience to take place, it is essential that those mentored have access to their mentors, and that the latter are available when needed.

Spontaneous, informal mentorship between two individuals (either within or outside an organization) have an impact equal to, if not greater than, that of any formal mentoring programs, since the choice to engage in the relationship is a spontaneous and wholly voluntary one. The protégé also enjoys the advantage of sharing common values on top of benefiting from the mentor's experience and teaching.

The best mentors, therefore, are those singled out by the aspiring leaders themselves, one mark of future leaders being their ability to identify and secure the aid of mentors (Devillard, 2001). Martine mentions the role that her spiritual mentors played by helping this business leader clarify her moral and social responsibility roles.

Mark explains the important guidance role that one of his mentors within his organization played at the very beginning of his career. Thanks to this mentoring, he chose to first get on-the-ground experience in a number of different areas, gaining a solid operational experience along the way before jumping into management roles. This unusual learning process prepared him more soundly for his current executive role.

The role of a mentor, therefore, is that of a guide, whose influence can be profound and long lasting. By providing guidance (see figure 5.2), the mentor allows learning to take place over an extended period through strategic reflection and well-grounded values.

To unleash your leadership capital, take it upon yourself to develop a mentoring relationship with a person of your choice who has solid life experience. Meet with this person from time to time to discuss your life views and projects, without developing a dependent relationship.

Are you yourself a formal or informal candidate for a mentoring role? Then give yourself this unique chance to develop another person's leadership capacity by deploying the three most important mentor's qualities: listening, asking insightful questions, and from time to time sharing lifelong perspectives.

The Coach

The leadership coach is an individual who provides aspiring leaders with specific advice and know-how concerning particular decisions, skills, tasks, and actions. The coach is more tactically oriented and teaches by means of instructions, advice, and feedback. The coach helps individuals to focus on specific situations, practices, or behaviors to develop or change.

Unlike that of the mentor, the coach's approach has a more immediate and practical perspective. It focuses less on developing a vision for the future, long-term goals, and self-knowledge. While the mentor supports others in the development of their own vision with a long-term perspective and by assisting them in identifying their values, coaches ask questions whose answers have a short or medium relevance to the leadership apprentice's interests and needs.

There are formal coaches who do this either as a profession or within the organization's coaching program. There are also informal ones, those who are more spontaneous, tending to emerge in particular situations and contexts.

A danger connected with this category of leadership actualization actor lies in the fact that certain individuals turn this role into something closer to the role of a psychologist or therapist without having any actual training in this area. Some of them even go so far as to provide diagnosis or set out therapeutic plans. Aspiring leaders, and those in charge of them, should pay careful attention to the approaches taken by their coaches.

Nevertheless, coaches, either formal or informal, can play a very important role in the lives of aspiring leaders by providing them with advice and instruction at the right times. The impact of good coaching is most evident when

- The two people in the relationship are willing participants who accept and respect each other.
- The coach provides useful, supportive, honest, and constructive feedback.
- The coach, in order to favor reflection and lasting learning, gives advice sparingly and in response to questions rather than giving all the answers straight away.

- The coach listens to and respects the coachee without judging the individual.

Let's look now at three different illustrations of coaching. In the first one, Helen is an informal coach who advised a young woman professional on how to handle the organization's politics, showing the do's and don'ts of the organization, how to make certain decisions, how to form alliances when necessary, and how to best exercise leadership in the context of an organization dominated by male managers.

The second example is the employer who acted as a very important coach to Harris, a future school manager. This employer regularly reviewed his school leadership and management tactics and strategies with him in order to help him learn lessons that could then be applied to future decisions.

Patrick, the third case, needed a coach who could make him more approachable in his relationships with the other team members. The coaching sessions followed a thorough evaluation of his management skills. Patrick benefited from a more formal type of coaching from a professional coach, who sat down with him and examined his abilities in terms of listening, interacting with others, interpersonal communication, emotional intelligence, and team motivation.

To benefit the most from coaching sessions, individuals need to take a positive attitude, be open to experiences, and pay attention during encounters, either formal or by chance, with people who could instruct and advise them. This requires a certain degree of humility, coupled with the ability to listen. Narcissistic individuals tend to benefit less from this type of learning, as, in their view, they are above instructions or advice.

So, coaches aid the development of leadership capital by providing their charges, either those who are just taking off or those who are more mature, with the opportunity to enhance more rapidly some of the skills needed to exercise leadership or to strengthen their existing leadership skills.

Pay careful attention to informal coaches that spontaneously assist you in developing your leadership capital. You can even take initiatives to meet with people who are willing to share with you their leadership know-how. But then again, you can also directly ask for a formal coach in order to develop specific leadership competencies such as assertiveness, strategic thinking and execution, negotiation, resolving disputes and conflicts, mobilizing teams, communication, planning and follow-up, change leadership, influence without formal authority, taking difficult decisions, intercultural communication, and any other leadership competencies.

Finally, if you are a potential leadership coach, offer your assistance but never impose it.

In the following pages, I illustrate the role of the challenger in actualizing leadership capital, which is a different role from those examined so far.

The Challenger

The challenger takes the individuals out of their comfort zone by

- Challenging them to excel in their current tasks.
- Increasing their roles within their current responsibilities.
- Assigning them to new, more demanding and complex tasks.

Challengers have a strong impact due to their pursuit of excellence. In their eyes, challenges given are not beyond the individual's abilities, even though they look more demanding than anything the group or individual has had to face previously. It is precisely because of challengers' beliefs in the abilities of those around them that challengers can play such an important role in leadership capital actualization. What follow are some real-life examples of leadership challengers.

Jack expects a high level of contribution from his colleagues, his partners, and those working under him, challenging those who are unaware of their own leadership potential. Some of his employees have been able to actualize their unexpected leadership capital as a consequence of his high expectations, while many others have fled, worried by the increasing demands, afraid of not being able to achieve the required standards or having or apprehending the sacrifice of personal time and effort in order to succeed.

Juan benefited from the influence of a leadership challenger at the very beginning of his career. At 25 years old, he was asked to negotiate the collective agreement for 3,000 employees, and to establish the firm's human resource management policies. Did he have any experience? No. Had he even demonstrated his negotiating skills in other situations? No. Without any experience in this area, and consequently, having no preexisting skills, he still accepted and faced up to the challenge. Some 30 years on, Juan still maintains that this experience was a real bonus in terms of the actualization of his leadership capital.

At the age of 40, Mary, a low-profile engineer, was placed in charge of a complex project that had encountered considerable difficulties in terms of delivery, quality, and production costs. Mary's new boss gave her this opportunity to prove herself. The confidence showed in her, Mary's combativeness uncovered by the situation, and her own technical expertise allowed her to put the project back on track. This experience, this moment of truth, allowed Mary to actualize the leadership potential that she had. Consequently, she was put in charge of other projects and, eventually, of an entire department.

The challenger provides challenging opportunities for people whom others would consider insufficiently experienced or not yet ready. In order to benefit a lot from the influence of a challenger, we must live up to the testing opportunities, take the chance of increasing our self-efficacy as a result of measuring ourselves against the task being offered, and have a certain confidence both in ourselves and in the challenger's judgment. We must also develop a certain amount of resilience to face a number of challenges along the way. Recall, this is the way in which development takes place; we build leadership by living up to challenges; we build resilience by facing adversity.

Challengers can sometimes have a habit of overtly displaying their impatience for and intolerance of underperformance, unfinished work, pointless arguments, and repeated mistakes. It sometimes happens that those working around some challengers prefer to distance themselves for different reasons. But consider instead the learning opportunity as a result of these heightened expectations, and the possibility to increase leadership self-efficacy and know-how.

As we have seen with Mary's example, these challenges provide opportunities for leadership actualization that are not limited to a single age group. However, when these powerful learning experiences take place at an early age, they are full of important lessons that benefit the individual for a lifetime. High schools, colleges, and universities as well as first jobs can be a tremendous learning ground for the development of leadership skills by providing important challenges and responsibilities. Challengers, therefore, are individuals who bring out our leadership potential through the challenges they set and the expectations they have of us.

As colleagues, immediate superiors, business partners, teachers, clients, and even parents, we can all play the role of challengers when we demand a higher standard in the work to produce.

These first three categories—the mentor, the coach and the challenger—generally work in a voluntary and deliberate fashion; they know consciously what they are doing. The influence of the next three categories—the passeur, the role model, and the anti-model—more often occurs without the actors being aware of their input.

The Passeur

The passeur is an individual who provides aspiring leaders with access to people, experiences, and information that will further develop their leadership capital. The passeur, taken from the French term for "boatman" or "ferryman," aids the progression of aspiring leaders from one stage to the next like a ferryman who transports travelers from one bank of a river to the other.

The passeur gives access to different opportunities and visions, allowing aspiring leaders to develop themselves in different ways. This passage, the access to the other side of the river, can significantly change the course of the lives of those able to take advantage of the opportunity the passeur provides.

Many aspiring leaders have come from organizational, family, professional, or other backgrounds that could do little to actualize their leadership or their aspirations. Passeurs allowed these individuals to change all of this.

An example of one such case is George L., whose employer played this role in his career when he was just a young office worker. This employer provided him with the opportunity to continue his studies in an international advanced training program at Chicago University. By doing so, this employer allowed George to gain a degree of knowledge in an area that would change his personal goals and values forever.

Teachers, professors, and other education professionals can easily play this role by providing information, by inviting lecturers to give testimonies, or by giving access to significant readings. For example, Martine's schoolteacher never saw the result of her input. Passeurs do just that without ever being able to measure their impact since their input can take either a short or a longer time to germinate. Passeurs see the direct impact of their role only when they get feedback later from accomplished professionals or leaders.

There are three different levels of passeurs:

1. Indirect and primary
2. Direct
3. Radical

The first of these groups consists of indirect passeurs, who introduce aspiring leaders to other passeurs. Teachers and education professionals act as indirect passeurs when they give access to information or people having a more visible and transforming influence. Managers play this role when they introduce their employees to powerful organizational members who will pass on key messages or information.

The second category level contains direct passeurs, who provide more direct access to leadership experiences or programs. Managers play this role when they free their employees so they can participate in different projects, jobs, or tasks.

The third level of passeurs is the most radical: the passeur takes an individual out of his or her own environment and integrates this individual into a world that is diametrically different to the one they have left behind. This offers the individual a completely new perspective on who they are and what they could achieve in the future. Again teachers and other resource persons in education environments exert this role when, for example, they provide projects for their students in a different school, neighborhood, or country. The same holds true in organizations when managers allow employees to work in a role totally different from what they have been trained in initially or when they give them the opportunity to work in a different country.

As you can see, many of us can be instrumental to others' leadership development. We never know what positive impact could come from our initiatives, thus the prescription not to shy away from sharing information and giving access to meaningful people. The same holds true in our own path to unleash our leadership potential; opening ourselves to information

Table 5.1. Passeurs, Actions, and Potential Impacts

Level	Actions	Potential Impacts	Examples
1. Indirect and primary	• Passing on critical information that will allow new experiences to take place. • Introducing the candidate to a person who will have a significant impact.	• Access to information, a person, or a program that will lead to significant development.	• Professor, teacher who provides information on an exchange program. • A person who introduces you to an expert, a model, or an influential individual.
2. Direct	• Allowing direct participation in experiences or job opportunities.	• Development of new competencies. • Self-confidence and self-efficacy improvements.	• A manager who assigns you to a new team or project (within organizational boundaries).
3. Radical	• Transporting the candidate out of his or her current world (social, cultural, professional), comfort zone, and providing new and different alternatives.	• Change in the way the individual sees his or her own future, world. • Discovery of new interests, talents. • Radical openness to new types of experiences.	• The direct supervisor who assigns the young professional to an international project or worldwide experience.

and people might bring unexpected and tremendous opportunities whatever the leadership level we are at.

Table 5.1 summarizes the different levels of passeurs, their actions, and the potential impact they each have.

The Inspirational Role Model

Human beings learn through direct or indirect observation of those around them, but also from written texts, historical accounts, and legends. This social learning takes place when we listen to, observe, and imitate models with whom we share interests, values, or aspirations. These role models can be found in our immediate environment or not, as we do not necessarily need to meet them in order to be inspired by their example. Aspiring leaders draw their inspiration from models whose characteristics they want to emulate.

The leaders I met throughout the years highlighted a number of different role models from whom they drew inspiration at different times in their lives. For some of them, their parents played this role. For others, a teacher or a family friend played this role in their development. Finally, as their horizons grew broader, they found more role models in other areas: at work, in politics, in the community, through religion, or in their leisure activities.

These role models can inspire those seeking to emulate them in both specific and more general terms. Their influence is clearest, firmest, and strongest when those following them have some idea, even if vague, of what it is that they want to do with their lives, their life purpose.

There are two dimensions to these role models: firstly, their visibility, and secondly, their accessibility. Their visibility relates to their presence in the individual's immediate environment (including time). Their accessibility relates to the degree to which the aspiring leader can be involved in actual direct meetings and discussions with them (see figure 5.2).

Familiar Models

The role models whose followers have the greatest opportunity to emulate them are those found in the followers' immediate surroundings.

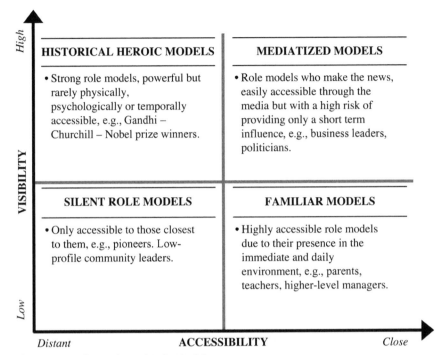

Figure 5.2. The Variety of Role Models

Individuals such as parents, teachers, team leaders, managers, trainers, work colleagues, and active community figures are all examples of potential role models in an aspiring leader's immediate environment. For this reason they are referred to as familiar models.

By listening to, observing, and imitating these role models, aspiring leaders can gain new knowledge and skills, clarify their interests and develop their talents. By comparing themselves to these leadership role models, they can determine their own potential.

For many leaders, their parents provided strong familiar models who allowed them to establish the basic values that provided the basis for their leadership. Maria's father, the Portuguese immigrant, passed his work ethic, his honesty, and his determination on to her. Martine's American mother, who was a community leader dedicated to improving the lives of those around her, inspired her greatly during the year she spent with her, aged 16.

Heroic and Historical Models

These models provide strong impact, but their potential to inspire can be limited by the temporal and contextual distances, combined with the fact that many of their heroic acts took place at unique moments in history. Nevertheless, their values, determination, and courage can still provide a source of inspiration. Gandhi, Churchill, Roosevelt, and Truman are examples of such figures. As well as providing leaders with inspiration in specific situations, biographies of these types of historical figures provide leaders with a great deal of inspiration in their working lives in general (Mintzberg, 2004).

Rudolph Giuliani (2002), the mayor of New York until 2002, states in his memoirs that, in the wake of the events of September 11, 2001, he drew inspiration from Churchill's determination to help Londoners in facing their adversity during the bombings of the English capital in the course of World War II.

Silent Role Models

These models are available only to a limited number of aspiring leaders. They are more discreet, and their influence tends not to extend beyond their own inner circle. This means that the potential for emulating them depends on whom they meet and what they pass on to their followers. In fact, only those around them even realize the scope of their contribution or their leadership. Researchers who work quietly in the background, community leaders, charity workers, and service leaders all fall into this category.

David Packard of Hewlett-Packard is one such example: he saw himself as being at the service of his employees, whom he viewed as partners; humility was one of his attributes (Collins, 2003). He refused to join the elite club of business directors, finding them greedy for increased profitability within their organizations to the detriment of their people: employees or community members. A number of aspiring leaders could benefit from getting to know these role models. Therefore, passeurs, mentors, and coaches could facilitate access to these role models.

Mediatized Role Models

The final category of role models is the complete opposite of the silent one. Members of this category are the mediatized role models, highly visible, and accessible through the media. They live in the same context, time, and space as those seeking to emulate them. They are the models made most accessible by the different forms of public media, but also by their activities within their own organizations. They provide an important source of inspiration precisely because of their contemporary nature, their accessibility, and the fact that they are widely known within their context. They can have a significant impact on those open to the example they provide. However, there is a risk of their influence failing to extend beyond the short term; the media can easily destroy their hero image.

The Anti-Model

Among the leaders I have met and coached, there are several who also describe the influence exerted on them by an anti-model present in their environment—someone they would go to any lengths to avoid emulating. These negative models might have a constructive impact on the development of their leadership capital by inspiring them to seek a different direction or to develop attributes and values that are the opposite of the ones displayed by these individuals.

Anti-models, therefore, can have a strong positive teaching impact on unleashing leadership by helping us to learn something about ourselves or how we want to lead our lives. One leader that I have met, for example, had her father as an anti-model. The women of Maria's native village were anti-models because of, as she explains, their apparent servility to men.

Anti-models can also have a negative teaching impact, when observers don't understand themselves better. This was the case, for example, for Henry and Francis, who entirely rejected their fathers as role models without clearly understanding what aspects of their behavior they objected to. As a consequence of this, they projected this conflicting relationship onto any situation where a similar paternal style of authority was present.

In his son's eyes, Francis's father was a domineering, intransigent financier whose only interest was in money. Without even understanding the true source of his dislike, Francis spent years living in a state of constant rebellion and rejecting any professional, accounting, or financial work that would remind him of his father until he finally realized that what he disliked about his father was his authoritarian and intransigent nature. He then realized that he actually enjoyed working with figures and being involved in the world of finance.

It is, therefore, important to clearly and precisely understand what it is about a given anti-model that repulses us in order to avoid rejecting not only all of their characteristics, but our own as well. Coaches and mentors can help aspiring leaders (and others) to form an understanding of their anti-models. Through better understanding and, consequently increased awareness, it is possible to release more energy and potential. By doing so, we can increase our own leadership capital and that of the people we work and live with.

As social beings, all individuals draw inspiration from other people. In the apprenticeship of leadership, six such roles played by important or influential individuals have been outlined in this chapter. Table 5.2 provides a descriptive summary of each role.

CONCLUSION

These six roles of potential leadership actualization educators are the most important ones. By directing, teaching, challenging, and inspiring aspiring leaders, leadership developers allow aspirations to emerge and provide lasting direction and guidance. Their influence depends largely on the willingness of leadership apprentices to actively engage with them and take steps to form a relationship with a mentor, coach, challenger, passeur, or role model.

Wishing to actualize your leadership capital, you should step forward and approach the people you feel might be beneficial to you in terms of leadership actualization or in achieving your purpose.

Actualizing our leadership capital means taking charge of our life, developing continuously an increased capacity to cooperate with others, mobilize, change things, and improve the quality of life of those around us, as well as our own. One aspect of this actualization is the search for significant, constructive, and supportive relationships.

Table 5.2. Leadership Developers: Summary

Role and Definition	Impacts
1. The Mentor Thanks to his or her vision, experience, and wisdom, the mentor directs, guides, questions, and encourages deeper reflection on certain leadership issues.	• Development of thought processes, philosophies on life, and instilling values. • Preparation for strategic life and career choices. • In some organizations, interventions on behalf of the protégé so that he or she might be assigned to better tasks and projects. • Learning the organizational values and culture.
2. The Coach The coach also provides guidance, but the object is more specific, aimed at the development of certain skills or making certain decisions in the short and medium term. He or she also provides instruction.	• Development of specific leadership skills. • Greater decision-making assurance. • A source of accompaniment at important moments.
3. The Passeur The passeur provides access to other individuals, experiences, and information that will make an important contribution to the emergence of leadership capital.	• Contact with individuals, information, or views of the world essential to the actualization of leadership capital.
4. The Challenger The challenger challenges his or her wards to improve themselves by providing them with difficult or demanding projects or new and complicated tasks.	• Accelerated skills development. • Development of leadership self-efficacy. • Increased capacity for taking certain calculated risks and breaking up routine.
5. The Anti-Model People like whom the aspiring leader does not want to become.	• Identification of your true values and aspirations. • The desire to do things better, differently.

Understanding the contribution of each of these distinct roles is two-fold. On the one hand, it helps you to become aware of these leadership educators, and to be more proactively receptive to their influence, actively searching for these kinds of relationships rather than passively waiting for chance to throw them your way. On the other hand, you can also liberate others' leadership potential by realizing any of these six roles.

6

Developing a Vision, a Purpose

People do not lack strength; they lack will. — Victor Hugo

A clear sense of direction enables a sailor to face courageously the bad weather and adverse conditions ahead while remaining alert in the face of the unknown quantities and the opportunities he encounters along the way. A vision plays the same role in developing our individual and collective leadership by providing meaning and purpose for our efforts and progress. Defining a vision and a purpose is the strategy presented in this chapter. Since vision is dynamic, and evolves over time according to maturity level and opportunities, this chapter illustrates also different categories of vision.

In a section of one organization, controversy erupted regarding a change in workload distribution. So, a group was invited to propose recommendations for improvements to the head of the division. The four group members are meeting for a fifth time, but after several hours of discussion, a consensus has still not been reached. The only thing that has changed is their level of frustration, with each member of the team feeling misunderstood by the others.

When the sources of their various disagreements are discussed afterward, it emerges that each member has very different professional, family, and personal objectives that shape their views on the possible solutions. There is no common goal, no shared understanding to unite them. Furthermore, each of them states that the only thing that brings them back to work each day is their salary. They feel that their work provides them with no great sense of professional satisfaction or stimulating social interactions. They also acknowledge, however, that the salary conditions and social benefits available to them in their current posts are better than those in the rest of the industry. For this reason, they wouldn't change jobs even if given the opportunity.

In another organization, a team of eight members is discussing a project for developing a communication tool for a new client. The tone of the discussion is dynamic, and each of the proposals put forward is discussed from all possible viewpoints. The time flies by, and lunchtime comes without anyone having requested a break in all morning. These employees are paid 20% less than their competitors, and their social benefits are the lowest in the industry, but their job satisfaction is still higher than that of the first group.

So what differences are there between these two groups? There are several, but the first and most important one concerns their goals. In the first group, there is no common goal to motivate and unite the group of individuals. Moreover, each of the group's members openly admits to having no motivation to come to work every morning other than their salary.

In the second group, each individual feels that he or she is contributing to the attainment of a clear and stimulating common goal: that of developing the best possible public communication concept for their client and, at the same time, ensuring the development of their young company. This vision, this shared goal, allows each member of the group to focus his or her best efforts and ideas on achieving it.

Having a personal goal has the same kind of motivational influence on an individual as these shared goals have on a group. Having an engaging and motivational personal goal helps individuals to focus their efforts, put distractions aside, and pour all of their efforts, time, and energy into realizing it. In terms of leadership capital development, having a goal—a sense of purpose that we are personally engaged in—is what mobilizes us and is also key to mobilizing others around our vision.

The aim of this chapter is to examine the influence of personal goals and vision on catalyzing leadership capital. This chapter goes beyond the usual perspective on the subject by offering a more detailed discussion on the energetic aspect of the goal and by providing a typology of visions and their links to the different stages of leadership maturity. Finally, this chapter offers some guidelines for identifying your own vision, at both the personal and collective levels.

Because the major unsuspected benefit of a vision lies in the power and vitality it provides, I present the parallel between vision, exercising leadership, and optimal experience, as defined by Csikszentmihalyi (1990), before exposing the typology of visions. But first let's clarify the meaning of vision, goal, and purpose.

VISION, GOAL, AND PURPOSE: DEFINITION

Vision defines a desired future and guides us in the actions necessary to create it. In itself, it represents a goal but with a concept of an idealistic future, and as the term indicates, with a certain picture of this future. A vision is something that we continuously work to achieve. Therefore, a vision

- Provides an image of a desired future.
- Appeals to both our aspirations and our needs.
- Represents a challenge that motivates a person or group to strive toward it.
- Aligns our personal and collective efforts.
- Helps each team member understand to what he or she is contributing.
- Provides guidelines in decision making.

Vision shared between team members, citizens, or organizational members builds a sense of commitment by providing everyone with a common representation of what it is that may be accomplished through concerted efforts.

A goal is derived from a vision, is more specifically targeted, and is more achievable in a short-term perspective. You can have a goal without having a vision, but this will require you to review your goals on a more regular basis, while you do not need to do this if you have a vision for the longer term. A goal has the following characteristics:

- It specifies what to do in order to realize your vision. It is more concrete.

- It is measurable; we know when it is achieved. Example: increase the safety measures by the end of this term.
- It is an end result in itself.

A purpose is similar to a goal but is usually referred to in the literature as the sense we want to give to our lives. In short, a vision defines a future while a goal defines the general actions required in order to realize this vision.

OPTIMAL EXPERIENCE AND GOALS

What causes individuals to spend long periods of time engaged in activities that provide no intrinsic reward? Csikszentmihalyi (1990), who has carried out extensive studies in this area, tried to answer this question by studying the behavior of chess players, sportsmen, artists, and skilled climbers. As it is clear that each of the groups studied enjoys its own particular activity, you have to ask why this is the case, and also why some of them are even willing to suffer in the course of these activities.

The interviews and observations carried out in the course of their studies revealed that the main source of motivation shared by all of the groups was the quality of their experiences during these activities. Several of them used the expression "flow" or "optimal experience" to describe what they felt. The term optimal experience refers to a state of consciousness, a state of mental fluidity and intense concentration on motivational and skilled activities, during which people feel completely absorbed by their activity to the extent that they lose all sense of time and location. They pay no attention to irrelevant details that could distract them from the task in front of them.

Csikszentmihalyi broadened his studies to include other categories of individuals from different backgrounds, cultures, and ages only to discover that optimal experience, although occurring most often outside the workplace, can also exist in the context of professional activities. Optimal experience has a significant impact in a number of areas, such as improved performance and creativity, increased skills development, higher self-esteem, and stress reduction.

There are eight key characteristics of this kind of experience. The first four of these concern the goals and tasks themselves:

1. Clear goals throughout the entire course of the activity. People having an optimal experience know exactly what they are trying to achieve at any given moment in the course of their activities. For example, climbers know what they have to do with each move to go higher; business directors have a clear vision of the next steps they need to take in implementing their business strategies in order for their plans to succeed.

2. Immediate feedback. In the course of an optimal experience, people receive a clear and immediate response to their actions. A cello player can tell right away whether or not she is playing well. This awareness of feedback, however, is dependent on another condition: having a clear goal.

3. A balance between the difficulty of the challenge and the individual's skills. During an optimal experience, people feel at once challenged by what they are doing and capable of succeeding due to the skills they possess. The task, therefore, requires a higher level of skill (making it a challenge) without being altogether unachievable.

The following aspects relate to the maximum level of concentration resulting from the characteristics mentioned above:

4. The exclusion of irrelevant information and distractions. The goal, the individual's attention to feedback, and the stimulating but realistic nature of the challenge provided by the task require that the individual's full attention be devoted to the activity. The musician pays no attention to the environment around him; the climber doesn't look up at the birds in the sky during these moments of intense concentration; and the worker doesn't get distracted by idle chatter.

5. No time is wasted worrying about failure. The climber concentrates so much on what she is doing that there is no time to worry about the risk she is taking. The business director or team leader focuses all of his attention on the task of achieving his goal and does not consider the possibility of failure.

6. Loss of self-consciousness. One thing that disappears during an optimal experience is the individual's self-consciousness, or worries about self, for example, clothing or opinions of others. During this type of experience, people "forget themselves." A lecturer is

too focused on relaying the message to worry about appearance or audience reaction.

7. Altered perception of time. People forget about the passage of time during optimal experiences. These periods of time can seem very long or very short due to the individual's extreme level of concentration. In a working team strongly focused on their task, the members can forget to take their breaks. The cello player mentioned earlier, in particular, will linger over her playing, and time seems to have slowed.

8. Finally, optimal experience is an autotelic (intrinsic) experience in which the activity becomes an end in itself rather than being the means to some other end.

In the first group described earlier, the workers did their job with the sole aim of gaining revenue. For them, their professional activity or daily working activities did not represent an end in itself. Their experience wasn't intrinsic; their goal wasn't grounded either within a vision or in the present and wasn't demanding of their skills. Once at work, these workers looked forward to only one thing: the day and the week ending as soon as possible.

In the second group, members shared clearly the goal to achieve: creating an innovative communication tool. They were clearly engaged in the activity for its own sake on top of aiming directly toward the goal targeted by each member and by the group as a whole. The pursuit of the goal required all their skills and thinking in order for them to create a new and innovative communication tool. The creative process gave them immediate feedback on the value and quality of an idea. They lost consciousness of time. In this latter group, leadership was shared among all of its members, with each of them contributing to the definition of parameters, proposal of ideas, and planning of subsequent stages. Their goal was shared, as was their involvement and enjoyment in doing the activities to get there.

Could self-leadership as well as shared leadership provide an optimal experience while mobilizing the maximum energy of members to achieve a common goal? Optimal experience and leadership have some very clear common elements. In fact, exercising leadership (which, as emphasized in the introduction, is different from management) shares many characteristics with the optimal experience described earlier, such as

- A clear goal.
- Focus and concentration to achieve the goal.
- Exercise of control by deploying necessary actions to succeed.
- Demanding of skills but yet possible.
- Regular feedback on progress.
- Less and less room for self-consciousness.
- Altered perception of time; for leaders in action mobilized by their goal, there are never enough hours in the day.

Whether working in business, the arts, education, or community or charity work, leaders are fully active and dedicated. They are guided in their everyday tasks, actions, and decisions by what constitutes both their own personal and collective goals. It is this vision of what they want or need to achieve, rather than the clock, that determines the manner in which they spend their time.

In the same way, people who are happy in their work or in their lives are those who have a very clear understanding of the goal they are working toward or the value of their work; just like a stonemason who understands that the work he is doing is not just breaking up rocks but contributing to the building of an entire cathedral.

This is also the essence of self-leadership; those who have already taken charge of their own lives are better equipped to motivate and involve others in working toward the same goal. Furthermore, being motivated by a personal vision, the leader—either alone or with the help of others—can develop a vision for an entire group, team, or organization. The following case clearly illustrates the way in which a clear goal, and the challenge it presents, can enable a person to access hitherto unknown leadership capital.

Robert Dutton is the president and CEO of RONA Inc., a Canadian public enterprise specializing in hardware and construction materials, employing over 25,000 people and with revenue of around $3.7 billion. In 2004, RONA was listed in the Financial Post as one of the firms most respected. Astonishingly, however, Mr. Dutton—who is now recognized as a great leader—has not always enjoyed confidence and success. The son of a hardware store owner, Robert Dutton was very timid in his adolescence and young adulthood. It was his search for a meaning in his life (a mission, a goal) that would act as an important catalyst to his leadership.

At the end of his studies at HEC Montreal, a business school, he was interested in marketing research, but his career ended up taking him in a completely different direction. In 1977, the then president of RONA insisted that Robert Dutton join the company, which at the time was just a small hardware cooperative. He accepted, although he initially had no intention of taking the position. This opportunity was to reveal a real passion in him for the world of hardware: its merchants, its members, its products, and the challenges it faced in an increasingly competitive world.

At key moments in his career, Robert Dutton would take time to reflect on the meaning of his life, the goal he was pursuing, and his professional, personal, and even his spiritual commitments. At the age of 26, he took time out to reflect on what elements should make up his mission and his personal moral code. In his eyes, this code had to reconcile his moral values with the company's search for profits.

Furthermore, it was becoming increasingly clear to him that he would need to become president of the company in order to guide its development in the right direction, motivate its employees, and ensure that its merchant members continued to feel pride in and a sense of belonging to the company. Service to merchants, employees, and clients, as well as their respect, dignity, and well-being, became the central pillars of his integrity-based moral code. Solidarity also became a guiding value in the firm's dealings with merchants, employees, clients, and suppliers.

Once again, at the age of 36, Robert Dutton took several months to reflect on his professional life in order to take stock of his life and its meaning. He further clarified the personal mission he wanted to achieve, which was to take place within RONA and was to bring together human, spiritual, and business values. In short, Robert Dutton's goal was to develop a profitable business in the context of a working environment where human values were at the heart of everything, even business decisions.

Since the days when he was a timid student, Robert Dutton was therefore able to actualize and exercise a level of leadership capital that no one would have suspected in the beginning, not even the man himself. Dutton succeeded in proving that he deserved to be placed among Canada's greatest business leaders (Girard, 2004). Much of this was due to the meaning he gave to his life, the vision and the goal he established for himself and for the company, and the way in which he went about his work. This allowed him to excel, motivate himself, and, in short, to actualize his leadership capital. Without his well-defined goals, he would probably have stayed in the shadows and would have been unable to surpass himself in the way he did.

Robert Dutton's leadership is marked by the same characteristics as the optimal experiences described earlier in this chapter: a clear goal, awareness of immediate feedback (appreciation from employees, clients, and merchants), a challenging task and a certain ability to rise to this challenge, and powers of concentration capable of ignoring tricks, artifice, distractions, and useless information. This experience led him to gradually lose the self-consciousness that had made him so timid in the past and allowed him to become a more open, welcoming, and sympathetic individual. The initial emergence of his leadership capital, however, took place as a result of the goal and the mission he set himself, and the different tasks he had to carry out in order to achieve these.

This is the case, to a certain extent, in all instances where leadership is exercised or actualized. The actualization of leadership capital in leaders occurs often as the result of a goal, initially expressed as a strong interest, set of principles, or guiding values. These goals then become clearer and more specific over time as a result of the various individuals' meetings, encounters, and experiences.

Personal vision is a major element of leadership actualization, even more important than the qualifications, talents, or skills you may possess. Each vision is unique and is the product of your reflections, history, interests, and your circumstances. However, a personal vision is not a static thing: it is dynamic, changing and evolving over time through an individual's encounters, needs, experiences, and personal reflections.

A vision shared among a group gives rise to the members' willingness to become involved, to rise through the ranks, to step out of their comfort zone or the security of their primary groups, to further develop themselves, and to face adversity.

How can a personal vision be clarified? Where does it come from? The clarification of a vision bringing meaning happens when we are confronted with a challenge, through a certain knowledge of ourselves, our interests, our talents, our values, and through meetings and events occurring in our life. The unleashing of our leadership capital can also take roots in a vision for a collective.

TYPOLOGY OF VISIONS

In the following pages, we reflect further on the idea of goals and personal vision by presenting a typology of visions. A vision can be fundamental, distinctive, and generative with impacts, intended or not, on a community, a profession, or an organization as it can transcend all types of groups by being supraorganizational or boundaryless. Whatever kind of vision it is (community, professional, organizational, or supraorganizational), it can still be fundamental, distinctive, or even generative (see figure 6.1).

This typology demonstrates that each vision is unique and varies according to scope, impact, and personal motives. The intent is also to highlight that the spectrum of visions for actualizing leadership capital in ourselves is unlimited. The first step is to draw one that will propel you forward, for your own benefit as well as for enhancing consequently or eventually the well-being of others. The objective of this next section is to provide you with a categorization of visions, illustrating its potential diversity.

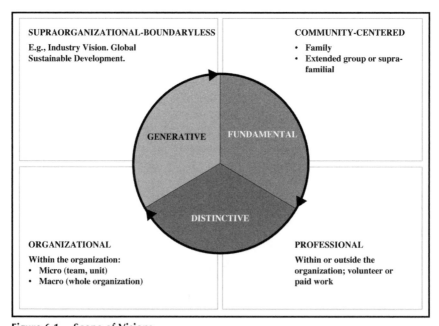

Figure 6.1.   Scope of Visions

Scope of Vision

First, four scopes of vision are presented. Each scope category has a distinct focus, from being specific to a community, an organization, or a profession to being boundaryless by transcending those three categories. The four categories of vision are

1. Community related
2. Professional
3. Organizational
4. Supraorganizational or boundaryless

Community Vision

A community vision has to do with a group of people and gives meaning to the lives of the members by allowing them to imagine what the community could be or how they might live in the future. The community vision aims at creating or improving the situation of a collective, small or large.

It can engulf an individual's immediate family or another specific group of people. For example, creating a family environment where each member of the family finds support to live up to their unique aspirations is a community vision. For many, this family type vision will give meaning and purpose to their lives for a specific period of time, when the children in the family are still dependent on the parents. This type of community vision is valuable but might not be enough to optimize leadership capital, as the more limited the scope of the vision, the more limited the actualization of leadership will be.

Other community visions extend beyond the limits of one's own immediate family. These extended community visions, which I call suprafamily vision, include other families or groups living the same challenges (e.g., school parents, autochthones, refugees, or elderly people) or in the same area (e.g., a district, town, or country). This wider community vision is found often with people who involve themselves in local, regional, or national community-based organizations.

For example, in 1980, the three community autochthonous (Innu) members on the north side of the St. Lawrence River, whom we talked about in chapter 1, came up with a unique vision for their community: give back their past pride to the community by helping it become entrepreneurial and financially independent from government subsidies or any other kind of social assistance. This vision was followed by a regularly updated action plan. Their vision has been achieved in less than 30 years.

Vision Related to Profession

A profession-related vision has to do with the purpose that involves one's profession, within or outside the limits of an organization. I define profession here in a broader sense, including all different types of work, volunteer as well as paid work, if the former involves the continuous use and development of professional know-how. The organization has less to do with that type of vision than the profession itself. While it includes as well the concept of community for whom the profession is exercised, the primary activator of the vision here originates in one's professional training and work-related occupation; for example, developing educational tools to make every math student succeed, or envisioning the development of a vaccine against cancer, or finding a cure for Alzheimer's disease.

A profession-related vision has its origins in a person's professional identity. Its development starts usually during the early years of an individual's professional life, as young professionals gain the experience they need to form a clearer idea of what they want to do and contribute. But it is not exclusive to any age group.

The better you can circumscribe your professional interests, the more you will invest time and efforts in professional training and experience and the more clearly you will be able to draw a profession-related vision. It was, in part, his profession and preparation as both an epidemiologist and a humanist that first allowed Dr. Mann to form a vision of his professional future, a vision that eventually extended to include the entire international community of AIDS sufferers.

In order for us to establish and live up this kind of vision, the profession that we practice must be closely related to our interests, talents, or abilities and even be a central aspect of how we define ourselves, professionally speaking.

Organizational Vision

Organizational vision is related to the future you foresee within the parameters of an organization. It is of a micro type when it has to do with a part of the whole organization such as a team or an administrative division. It is a macro-organizational vision when the scope involves the entire organization.

Vision for a team, or micro-organizational vision, is related to the future of a team, a department, or a division, building on its shared aspirations and interests, achievements, cohesion, strengths, and the specific community it serves.

In the team mentioned at the very beginning of this chapter, it was partly the absence of this kind of team vision that created the collective lack of motivation and constructive energy, while there were no such problems in the second group studied. In this second case, the team's micro-organizational vision was also linked to the entire company's vision. Team members were very clear about what they envisioned for the team and how it was linked to the firm's organizational vision. Viewed in this way, the vision became even stronger and provided greater motivation as it appealed to their collective goals and provided them with a sense of belonging. As in the case of optimal experience, the goal in question has to appeal to the group's intrinsic motivations rather than material or financial rewards, which the first group was locked into.

Macro-organizational vision concerns the future of an entire organization. It synthesizes the potential future of an organization, appealing to the organization members' aspirations and sense of pride in their work. Employees who take pride in their work usually perform at higher levels and deliver better results. This is true for all kinds of organizations. The challenge then is to define and articulate a mobilizing vision, capable of getting everyone to give their best. At the organizational level, the principles guiding the vision have to represent values shared between the organization's members. For illustration purposes, here are a few examples of two organizational visions:

- Creating a school learning environment where all students see their worth and learn to realize their full potential.

- The Nucor company's vision as stated on their website: "To be the safest, highest quality, lowest cost, most productive and most profitable steel and steel products company in the world. We are committed to doing this while being cultural and environmental stewards in our communities where we live and work. We are succeeding by working together" (Nucor, Inc., 2008).

Organizational visions, when defined by the people who will live it, have more power and impact than when it is done behind closed doors. This is true for any kind of organization. In schools, teachers, students, management, and parents can all be consulted. When this is done, the vision outlives the temporality of individuals.

Supraorganizational or Boundaryless Vision

This final category provides a vision on a grander scale. It transcends an organization to encompass a cause of a grander nature. It is transorganizational, transborder, boundaryless.

This kind of vision governs greater leaders. Gandhi's, Martin Luther King's, or Roosevelt's vision belongs to this category. Gandhi's vision was to bring peace and democracy for all people whatever their class and status. King's vision was initially stated in 1957 in the newsletter of the newly formed Southern Christian Leadership Conference (Smith & Zepp, 1974), where he describes the purpose and goal of that organization as follows: "The ultimate aim of SCLC is to foster and create the 'beloved community' in America where brotherhood is a reality. . . . Our ultimate goal is genuine intergroup and interpersonal living—integration."

Realizing our great world interdependency, examples of supraorganizational visions will hopefully abound more and more: to bring peace, eradicate epidemics, raise education levels of women, protect wildlife and endangered species, and so on.

Levels of Visions

On top of having a different impact such as community based, profession related, organizational, or supraorganizational, a vision can be also be fundamental, distinctive, or generative.

The four categories of visions can have three different degrees of depth or maturity: fundamental, distinctive, and generative. This depends on the individual's maturity, needs, and circumstances. The actualization of leadership capital is optimized when the vision is grounded in all the three vision levels. Reflection time can assist you not only in clarifying your vision but also in bringing it from one vision level to the other.

Leaders have goals that change or become clearer over time. Some have a vision of the status they want to have within their organization, such as becoming the head of a division or of an entire firm. Others have visions based on their personal values and principles, such as being of service to others, gaining respect or recognition, or becoming financially independent. Yet others develop a vision based partly or wholly on the needs of one particular group. In a nutshell, the different levels or depths of visions can be summarized as follows:

1. A fundamental vision is based on our fundamental values and principles.
2. A distinctive vision is based on our awareness of our particular talent, added value, or interest.
3. And a generative vision is based on our desire to increase the well-being of a particular group or of future generations, or to make a lasting contribution.

Each of these visions responds to a specific question and has its own specific impacts.

Fundamental (Value-Based) Vision

This level of vision is related to the fundamental values and principles that provide us with guidance throughout our entire life. For some, their fundamental vision focuses more on the self—for example, being financially independent, being respected, or being productive. For others, their founding vision is more concerned with the relationship with a specific group or community, such as improving others' well-being, encouraging cooperation between different groups, helping those less fortunate, and so on.

Our leadership potential is maximized through self-knowledge, and part of it is knowing our true values and our guiding principles in life. The deeper our reflection on our fundamental values and principles, the more we are able to make decisions based on these and be engaged in the courses of action we choose and live with their consequences.

As an example, let's look at an episode in the life of Katharine Graham, board chairman and CEO of the *Washington Post* from 1973 to 1991. She was faced at a crucial time with the choice between publishing a Department of Defense report on the Vietnam War or keeping it quiet and avoiding the hostile reaction that the U.S. government would undoubtedly have to its publication. This publication was covering what became known as the Watergate scandal.

In fact, she says in her memoirs, she was faced with a choice between economic survival or remaining faithful to her own values and the spirit of her free independent business. She elected to stay true to her values. Her values guided her decisions, allowing her to display an act of leadership and to face adversity that usually comes with it. Nevertheless, the end result was that her newspaper grew in stature and became highly respected by its readers (Graham, 1997).

A fundamental vision can arise at any point in life. The answers that individuals provide to these questions, whenever they face them, allow them to better select the opportunities before them, decide courageously, and live by their choices.

A fundamental vision is, as its name indicates, one that provides a basis for other levels of vision. The clearer, stronger, and better defined this primary vision is, therefore, the stronger the generative vision based on it will be, and the more leadership capital will be activated.

Below are some of the questions whose answers provide the basis for defining your own fundamental vision (see table 6.1). The formation of this vision represents the first stage of maturity in a leader's actualization.

Ideally, these fundamental values, which are a key constituent of a fundamental vision, should include elements relating to the individual (such as courage or independence) and to dealing with others (e.g., honesty, respect, or solidarity). At the collective level, a group can also define its fundamental shared values. As with the vision and the goal, common values provide a sound basis for shared leadership to happen.

Table 6.1. Proposed Questions for Defining a Fundamental Vision

At the individual level:

1. What do you think are your guiding principles in life?
2. Suppose you have the choice between two jobs corresponding to both your needs and your expectations; what criteria will you use to guide your decision?
3. Think about a successful project, an achievement, or a difficult but good decision you have made. What values guided you in this project or achievement?
4. What do your goals, values, and the basis for your actions and achievements say about you?
5. By looking at the answers you gave to the previous questions, what can you conclude about your priorities from the way you lead your life?
6. Summarize in a few sentences how you want to lead your life based on your values and guiding principles.

At the collective level:

1. What are the values that the different group members share? Address and discuss these values.
2. Think of a project, a success that the group achieved. What made the group proud?
3. In 3–5 years from now, your group meets to discuss its accomplishments. Imagine those accomplishments. What are they? What principles guided the actions and decisions to realize those realizations?
4. Who are the different stakeholders of the group's raison d'être (e.g., parents, students, employees, community members, etc.)? What do they expect from you in terms of performance, services, or products?
5. Summarize in a few sentences the future of your group. What does it look like? What will be your guiding principles to realize that future?

Distinctive Vision

A distinctive vision is one that stems from our understanding and awareness of our talents, defined here as what constitutes not only our strengths but also our interests, our unique history and experience. A distinctive vision is therefore the distinctive value and quality each of us brings to this world. Self-knowledge is necessary to form a vision of ourselves in the future and to understand the specific contribution that we offer. It can also give us the confidence to act in situations that require our own particular kind of input.

Individuals within organizations, teams, or collectivities are more likely to show leadership when they fully understand the importance of their contribution to their group. They are more likely to remain passive and carry out their tasks without any real enthusiasm when they have not yet formed this distinctive vision of themselves. This is the reason why teachers, trainers, coaches, and team leaders have an important role in developing students', participants', and employees' confidence in their value, in the richness of their uniqueness, their contributions as well as their ideas.

Developing our leadership capital as well as developing others' leadership requires taking all the steps necessary to define that distinctive vision.

It is up to us to form our own distinctive and motivational vision; it doesn't necessarily require having any exceptional talents. Imagine what spending 5 or even 10 years or more, working on our real interests would allow us to achieve in comparison to what we would achieve in the same period spent working on repetitive tasks for which we have no real motivation.

A distinctive vision can take shape during the early stages of forming a social identity when adolescents consider who they are, what they like, what they want, and what sets them apart from their parents and their peers. While part of this vision is discovered during adolescence, however, it continues to be developed and strengthened throughout our life as a result of our interests, experiences, encounters, observations of ourselves and our environment and, of course, through the opportunities that come our way. It is therefore possible for a distinctive vision to be developed at any age.

A personal vision related to our talents and interests releases boundless reserves of energy and consequently, our unique leadership. Since leaders are as varied as they are unique, it is up to us to discover, sometimes with the help of others, where our true interests and talents lie. No one else can do it for us. Although this discovery can occur in different ways depending on the individual involved, there are two main lines of enquiry that are worth following:

1. Exposing ourselves to different experiences and, consequently, to different views of the world as early as possible. This allows the discovery of new areas of interest, meeting people with different backgrounds, needs, interests, and talents.
2. Developing one or several of the interests that arise spontaneously within us and that provide us with a real sense of enjoyment or accomplishment. This is generally the course taken by inventors, artists, researchers, community activists and organizers, and entrepreneurs.

Table 6.2.   Proposed Questions for Defining a Distinctive Vision

1. What are your interests? What do you most like and dislike doing? Are these activities related to research, planning, or implementation? Are they related to the arts, science, business, health, social sciences, engineering? Do you prefer to work alone or as part of a group? Would you like to work locally, in another region, or even in another country?
2. Which of these above activities generally gives you the most satisfaction, pride, sense of accomplishment, and optimal experience?
3. What are your talents? What really sets you apart? What unique contribution do you like to make? What can you do to develop this talent or interest?
4. What competencies do you have? What qualities distinguish you?
5. Is there a current need or demand in society that could be satisfied by this talent or interest? What is it? What can you do to identify and better understand it?
6. In a few sentences, describe how you see your future contribution, let's say in 3 to 5 or 10 years from now.

It is through curiosity and openness to others, combined with a process of social comparison, that individuals are able to discover their own talents and interests.

Forming a distinctive vision based on a fundamental vision, however, represents the second stage of maturity in leadership capital actualization, as it is based on a greater level of self-understanding. A distinctive vision that does not have its roots in a fundamental vision runs the risk of encouraging arrogance and the growth of a kind of narcissism. On the other hand, a distinctive vision gets more powerful when it rests on fundamental values that are collectively embedded in the good of a group.

Table 6.2 proposes questions related to the definition of a distinctive vision.

Generative Vision

The term generative refers to the psychological phenomenon of generativity, a term coined by Erik Erikson (1993) to describe the concern of establishing and guiding the next generation. Generative vision is inspired by the heritage we want to leave for other generations. It is developed by our thoughts and dreams of what life will be like for future generations. These generations could be related to members of our immediate family. However, this vision more often relates to completely different groups such as groups of citizens, employees, members of a particular profession, underprivileged groups in society, or nonprofit organizations.

This generative vision is in some way related to a higher level of maturity in leaders. It tends to occur when they arrive at a point in their lives when they want to contribute to the sustainable development either of their own organization or of other groups in society.

What legacy do you want to leave behind and to which groups' needs? Which accomplishments will leave you feeling satisfied with your life when you look back on it? These are the questions pertaining to a generative vision definition.

Obviously, a strong and well-defined generative vision is not something that most people possess at the beginning of their adult lives. In fact, individuals must first have a certain openness to the world around them in order to fully understand its challenges and needs. They have to emerge from the identity-searching phase of young adulthood to become more aware of and connected to the needs of their social environment and to the role that they can play in it. Or they may have been exposed to the needs of others in a different way.

For example, it is in part a generative vision to build a better world that motivates leaders like Bill and Melinda Gates through their foundation, or Mohammad Yunus, Nobel Peace Prize laureate, through his microcredit banking, to enable the poor and the poorest to live in a world without poverty.

A generative vision doesn't have to wait for old age to take form. This can be exemplified by two Nobel Peace Prize winners in 1976, Betty Williams, a Protestant, and Mairead Corrigan, a Catholic. At the age of 22 years, they cofounded the Northern Ireland Peace Movement directed at ending the violence in Northern Ireland between religious rivals groups (see NobelPrize.org, 2008).

In fact, all those who work to improve the quality of others' lives and who contribute in their own way to leaving a healthier environment for younger or future generations are displaying leadership brought about by this kind of generative vision. At the heart of any generative vision is the desire to have a positive and lasting impact on future generations. The strength of this vision and the individual's engagement in it determine the extent of the subsequent effort at make it a reality.

In our increasingly individualist and narcissistic Western societies, leaders with a generative vision are in increasingly short supply considering the extent of our need for them. Every leader and every society should seek to

Table 6.3. Proposed Questions for Defining a Generative Vision

1. What are the most important groups in society for which you wish a better future?
2. Which scenarios, positive or negative, are conceivable for the future of these specific groups: adolescents in the area, school pupils, refugee families, work teams, professional communities, organizations, and so on?
3. What needs to be done, collectively and individually, to obtain a positive outcome?
4. What has to be done to prevent the negative outcome from occurring?
5. Which individual and collective acts of leadership will provide them with a better future?
6. What could you do and with whom?
7. In a few sentences, describe how you see your future contribution, let's say in 3 to 5 or 10 years from now.

develop this kind of generative vision, while educators of all kinds (teachers, trainers, coaches, parents, mentors, passeurs, and consultants) should help to clarify this type of vision by listening to their charges, asking them the right questions, and putting these prospective leaders in contact with people who have different perspectives and those who can highlight collective needs, a sense of duty, and their potential contributions. Table 6.3 presents a few questions to guide you in developing a generative vision.

Visions, driven by a desire to contribute to a better future for you, your community, or future generations, are varied in nature.

CONCLUSION

Contrary to popular ideas, many leaders, to begin with, did not have a very clear idea of the course to give to their lives. What they did usually determine to a certain degree, however, was the basis of a fundamental vision. They were also open to any opportunities, demands, and encounters that came their way. They kept a balance between, on the one hand, controlling the direction they wish their lives to take and, on the other hand, maintaining a degree of flexibility in order to cope with the different people, challenges, and circumstances they found themselves encountering.

A vision transforms itself many times in a lifetime. Aspiring leaders have to tackle the paradox of staying on course to realize their visions while also remaining flexible enough to be open to any opportunities that they are presented with.

Having personal vision, meaning, and direction in our life—something that is so difficult to establish and yet so essential to leadership capital actualization—must also work in tandem with a constant openness to new experiences and opportunities.

Finally, forming a vision allows us to develop an optimal level of leadership capital, as the visualization of our aspirations exerts both a self-pressure to realize it and an extremely powerful force of attraction on others. This works both at the individual or collective levels.

7

Getting into Leadership Actions and Engagement

Even if a man (or a woman) died at the age of hundred years and not turned his aspiration into reality, it would still be considered an early death.—Chinese Maxim

In the end, leadership is actualized and developed mainly through experiences and action. As Mandela said, a vision without action is no more than a dream. You don't yet have a vision or a purpose to achieve? No matter, being proactive by seizing opportunities and answering calls of duty contributes not only to leadership development but eventually to vision building.

A large number of the leaders studied, through interviews, observations, and biographies, did not have as high a level of leadership self-confidence or self-efficacy at the beginning of their careers. In fact, a number of them were not particularly sure of themselves to begin with. This changed, however, as a result of the experience they were able to gain through the challenges they accepted and the opportunities they encountered. According to leaders themselves, getting into action is the best method for developing leadership capacity, as one learns to be a leader by serving as a leader.

So far, I have presented six strategies to activate the leadership potential in you and in groups. This chapter presents the seventh one: getting into action. Three different sets of actions that can trigger leadership development are described, along their corresponding commitments:

1. Actions in line with your vision or purpose and the dedication to fulfill them.
2. Actions that come with stepping out when facing current challenges and opportunities, and the commitment to do your best.
3. Actions that come with a call of duty, and the sense of obligation to honor it.

The next section reviews how leadership is developed and actualized through these three forms of action and engagement.

ACTION AND ENGAGEMENT TO FULFILL A VISION

For Joseph-Armand Bombardier, the snowmobile inventor and its first manufacturer, creating a vehicle able to travel over snow and hostile terrain was an initial dream. His ambition, early on in life, was to conceive a vehicle that could go on snow, transporting patients, students, and citizens during wintertime. He succeeded in 1937 by producing a sort of car on tracks and skis, called the B-7, and by establishing a Canadian manufacturing giant along the way. Through his dream, actualized in his everyday efforts, Bombardier changed the way we travel over snow (MacDonald, 2001).

His vision of a future vehicle became a reality through action, that is to say, as a result of many years of research, planning, prototypes, and trials. From the age of 15 years, he devoted most of his time, efforts, and money to his personal engagement in the project, and to the realization of his aspirations as an inventor. It took him 13 years before seeing its realization. Once he had obtained the patent for his snowmobile, he continued along the same path by creating and producing new vehicles (MacDonald, 2001), notably different traction vehicles such as the well-known traction snowmobile and the Muskeg Tractor, a type of vehicle capable of traveling on hazardous terrain due to its lack of pressure on the ground.

Actualizing leadership capital through a vision or purpose essentially means acting in accordance with our aspirations. More specifically, it means identifying a goal and taking the action required to achieve it. Along the way, it develops our talents, interests, and skills. And the very fact that we have taken action with a clear direction and goal can be one of the major keys to leadership actualization.

There are many other examples of entrepreneurs, community leaders, writers, creative individuals, musicians, and everyday citizens who make the decision to lead their lives according to their own unique purpose. The purpose can have both a personal and a collective view. These people truly follow their aspirations and the life choices that come with them. By doing this, they allow their leadership to grow and reveal itself through the actions and results achieved. Their actions not only contribute to their own personal development but also have a tremendous potential for the economic, social, environmental, or cultural development of society.

The Benefits of Vision-Based Action

The benefits of actualizing our vision through actions bring coherence, self-motivation, and an increased capacity for mobilizing others. Each of the three aspects has a dynamic effect on the other. Coherence between vision and action impacts on our own self-mobilization and influences us to move continuously in that direction. In turn, this self-mobilization and energetic coherence inspire and mobilize others to follow our path.

Coherence means that there is a synchronicity between who we are, what we would like to become, and the actions and steps we are taking to get there (see figure 7.1). The coherence between these three factors releases the energy, strength, and motivation required to act, to overcome challenges, and to tackle obstacles. Knowing ourselves is an essential condition for achieving coherence, as we have to be aware of our strengths, our weaknesses, and above all, our aspirations.

Once we have found this coherence between who we are, what we aspire to, and what we are actually doing, we can rest assured that we are on the right path toward actualizing our leadership potential. This coherence provides us with everyday and long-term motivation to make these aspirations and goals a reality.

When this synchronicity does not exist and when we are not in concordance with our true selves, goal, or purpose (interests, motivations,

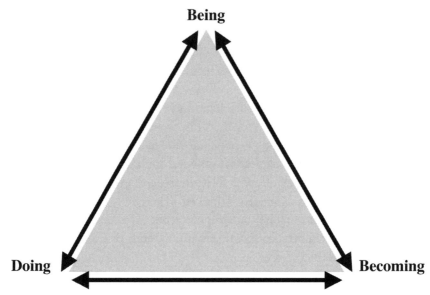

Figure 7.1. Coherence between Doing (Action), Purpose (Becoming), and Self (Being)

aptitudes, values), we become more and more passive; we feel frustrated, helpless, and resentful as well as lacking a sense of accomplishment. It is like a boat not having its tiller. Our time is spent waiting for something to entertain us or distract us: new tasks, new people, hoping that the future will be more enjoyable than the present—the weekend, our holidays, and even our retirement years. We risk being the followers of others, more inclined to obey, follow, or conform.

This passivity can transform itself into aggressiveness, either toward others or toward ourselves. Hostility toward others can take on many forms: falling onto rumors regarding others, criticism, resentment, rejection, verbal aggression, and so on and so forth. Self-inflicted aggression can take on different forms: self-criticism, distraction, alcohol or food abuse, affective dependencies, drug and eating disorders.

Those possessing coherence and displaying personal motivation attract others who are willing to follow them. Their dynamism influences, convinces, and motivates others. Their genuine coherence and personal motivation catalyze others to move in a certain direction, to overcome their limits and achieve a greater project. Acting in coherence with what we are, motivating ourselves, and, in short, actualizing our leadership capital also allow us to surround ourselves with individuals prepared to join us in our long-term project.

This is not to say that finding this coherence is easy; actually, it requires a lot of thought, reflection time, and action. Personal motivation is undoubtedly a major benefit of coherence, releasing a hitherto latent source of energy.

Unleashing our unique leadership capital can happen through vision-based actions, but it can also occur due to decisions or initiatives taken in face of unexpected opportunities we encounter. This second category of action is the object of the next section.

ACTION AND ENGAGEMENT BY SEIZING OPPORTUNITIES

For some people actualizing leadership capital happens when, responding to the demands of a particular situation or to a group's request, they step outside of their comfort zone. Developing leadership capital can happen because we take initiative to seize, materialize, or resolve an opportunity or a need we see. The opportunity is there and we are the one ready to make it a reality. This is how Ray Kroc built the first McDonald's restaurant.

Ray Kroc was a salesman, selling cups across the United States. As related by Pepin (1998), a journalist for *Time* magazine, Kroc noticed, on his travels, a remarkable restaurant in San Bernardino, California, owned by two brothers, Dick and Mac McDonald. The brothers had produced a very limited menu of hamburgers, fries, soft drinks, and milk shakes. Amazed by the effectiveness of their operation, he started thinking about building McDonald's stores all over the United States. At 52 years old, he saw an opportunity, envisioned a future in a certain manner, then exploited this idea by virtue of developing a sophisticated operating and delivery system supported by advertising programs.

Life paths are seldom linear; actions and encounters take us to unsuspected destinations. The life journey offers surprises, deceits, struggles, and rewards. Seizing opportunities, responding to challenges, and even taking risks can be important steps toward leadership actualization. Taking action, stepping out, or just doing it opens other doors, and brings with it other opportunities.

Even if it is within a certain large range of activities, all leaders that I meet, coach, study, or interview emphasize a certain nonlinearity in their life, highlighting the need for flexibility and a certain openness to opportunities and encounters. Of course, some had a certain idea of their fundamental vision, such as giving support to cancer patients, manufacturing snowmobiles, giving dignity to a group, leading a business, eliminating poverty; but the intricacies weren't that specific. What was clear though is that they have grasped opportunities when the moment came; they have taken on challenges facing them; they have faced their fears with courage and commitment.

A third category of action that can trigger leadership development has to do with the sense of duty.

ACTION AND ENGAGEMENT
TO ANSWER A CALL OF DUTY

The following example demonstrates the undeniable role played in leadership capital actualization by action following a call of duty. At the age of 50, Sheila Kussner (personal communication, May 2002) was a dynamic lady, dedicated to her family and her local community, married to a businessman, and living comfortably in her suburb. Having witnessed what little information and support was given to cancer victims and their families when her husband was himself struck by this disease, she decided to set up an organization called Hope and Cope, with the mission of providing support for patients and those close to them.

The life story of Sheila Kussner is characterized by her sense of responsibility for her own life. Until her adolescence, Sheila led a normal life. She was an intelligent girl, surrounded by a loving group of family and friends. At the age of 14, however, her life took a dramatic turn: she suddenly learned that she had contracted bone cancer and that she had only a 5% chance of 5-year survival. At that time, in 1946, the treatment options available today, such as radiotherapy and chemotherapy, did not yet exist.

The only way to save her life and let her be part of the 5% of people who survive this type of cancer was to amputate the affected leg at the knee. The following weeks and months were filled not only with the trauma of amputation but also with unendurable physical pain. There was also a profound change in her as she now formed the image of herself as "infirm" and became ashamed of her body. Fortunately, her parents provided her with her first lesson in survival and, perhaps, in leadership: to accept herself as she was and to overcome the physical and social difficulties facing her; to grow and develop, pursuing her interests, aspirations, and talents.

Her adaptation to this new situation happened in stages, as she progressed from denial to rejection to eventual acceptance of her handicap. By focusing on her strengths rather than on her limitations, on the options open to her rather than those she had lost, she made the choice to put aside her bitterness and to become a better person. Her illness and the trauma she had suffered had given her a profound sense of empathy and compassion for others, and for amputees in particular. Little by little, she found herself being asked to visit other patients and to show them that it was still possible to have a happy life despite amputation and serious illness.

Twenty years after her marriage, her life was hit by a new shock: her husband contracted lymphoma and was given very little chance of survival. For two years, he underwent radio and chemotherapy. Finally, a long period of remission began. Little by little, Sheila began to receive calls from people all over North America asking her for advice on the treatment her husband had received, about specialists, and about the various resources available.

In 1980, the word cancer was still taboo, and there were not yet any programs in place to support patients or their families through this ordeal. Sheila became aware of the need for a support service to provide a listening ear and practical advice for others battling this illness. This was her call to duty, a sense that she must do something for others.

Following her husband's recovery, Sheila Kussner decided to act. Firstly, she engaged herself, her friends, and her acquaintances in establishing a resource center run by volunteers. Their efforts were initially received with skepticism by hospital officials. How could people not trained as health specialists offer such services? they asked. However, thanks to her determination, her actions, and the help of others, Sheila opened one such resource center in 1981.

Initially consisting mainly of volunteers, it is today staffed by qualified social workers and counselors. The Hope and Cope resource center is an independent program recognized as a pioneer among cancer support groups.

This center has given rise to other similar establishments in a number of different locations worldwide. The results of research carried out in the center on the psychosocial aspects of support for patients and their families have been published in scientific journals. Sheila Kussner's actions have also led to the creation of the Department of Oncology at McGill University.

Sheila Kussner's example clearly illustrates how the call of duty, which was the sense of having to help others in need of support and information on cancer, expanded her leadership potential and benefited thousands of people. Her call of duty became a vision, setting a Hope and Cope program. And then all her efforts and her actions converged to achieve it, making it a reality through a high level of commitment.

But why, if the leadership development's benefits are so great in terms of personal development, of energy producing and the impacts it has on others, aren't there more people getting into action either to realize their vision, seize opportunities when they come our way, or answer from time to time the call of duty? The next section proposes some answers.

BARRIERS TO ACTION AND ENGAGEMENT

Several barriers can contribute to the difficulty in pursuing our destiny, taking control of our own life or of situations, seizing leadership opportunities, or answering the call of duty, and consequently actualizing thereafter our leadership capital. The main obstacles to full engagement and action are

1. Fear of the unknown
2. A lack of motivational personal vision
3. A shortfall between our aspirations and prevailing social trends
4. Insufficient self-confidence and self-efficacy
5. Weakened resilience
6. Self-victimization
7. Idealization of leaders and the sense of our own imperfection

These obstacles, which cause us to limit ourselves in actualizing our own leadership capital and becoming the scriptwriters and scene-setters of our own lives, are explained in the following pages. Steps that can be taken to overcome these obstacles are also proposed.

Fears

Sometimes, we justify our refusal to define our own personal vision or to take on opportunities because of our fears: fear of having to act to realize it; fear of the difficulties, frustrations, and failures that this could potentially involve; fear of the unknown and the uncertainty, not knowing what the outcome will be. We might even apprehend the risk of failing, or what's more, the risk of succeeding with a cascade of further expectations and responsibilities. Letting fear leads us is the poison of leadership.

There are numerous strategies to address this barrier to action and engagement, but the key leitmotifs are to face our fears and "just do it," to recognize that fear is part of living, and that all leaders have to overcome their own from time to time. Recall also that there is nothing to fear more than fear itself (Roosevelt, 1933) and that getting into action is the antidote to fears; the more we face our fears, the less frightening they become. Make a list of your fears, and for each fear, determine an action to take. Consider for some doing just the exact opposite of what you are fearing. Finally, make sure to congratulate yourself just for making an attempt, whatever the outcome of your actions is.

Lack of Motivational Personal Vision

Other times, we shy away from defining a vision because we think it has to be grandiose or that it has to make us a hero leader. In reality, a vision is just how we project ourselves in the future, be it the near or distant future. And this projection originates from many variables: interests, perceptions of collective needs, talent, desires, motivations, current and upcoming challenges, or values. This medium- or long-term engagement with a vision can seem daunting, but in reality a vision is neither static nor unchanging. In fact, a vision is developed over time and is guided by experience. It is in this way that a leader's original project evolves on a pace with the experience gained, the feedback received, and the resources available.

Having a motivational vision and acting to realize it brings increased personal well-being through the energy and pleasure it generates, not only when it is fully realized but also with each step taken toward it. Therefore, the first step in addressing this obstacle is to actively define a vision. Just as putting on your running shoes is a great step to launching a fitness activity, drawing a few lines of a possible vision is the very first action to take. And review this first draft over time.

Shortfall between Our Aspirations and Prevailing Social Trends

It happens all too often that our social environment does not provide us with the support we need to realize our visions or aspirations, whether in terms of openness or by luring us into leisure pursuits or a collective state of inaction.

At the outset, Sheila Kussner received no support or encouragement from the medical establishment. J.-Armand Bombardier was considered eccentric, and was mocked during the various trials of his early prototypes. Parks, Gandhi, and Mandela were jailed among other things. Mohammed Yunus overcame administrative blockages, mistrust, and mockeries from the financial world, and fear and panic from the poorest themselves.

In organizations, various groups develop the sense of having little influence as result of coercive or paternalistic management styles, regular staff cutbacks aimed at boosting the firm's profits, and organizational conflicts of all kinds. This feeling of collective helplessness leads usually to individual inactivity, paralysis, demotivation, dissatisfaction, and self-pity. In other words, belonging to a helpless group can endanger the individual potential for leadership development and practice unless we take action.

Taking action in face of this type of obstacle involves neutralizing the negative influence the group has on us by having more constructive relationships with certain key members, taking steps to modify the group's pessimistic discourse such as addressing it or reframing constructively the discourse, raising the issue, asserting our point of view and ideas, or even changing or joining other more constructive groups or organizations.

Insufficient Self-Confidence and Self-Efficacy

Failing to believe in our own ability to succeed despite effort and perserverence is a significant obstacle to action. However, even a lack of self-efficacy can be overcome when we connect a vision, a purpose, or objectives with our aspirations and interests. Engagement allows us to lose our self-consciousness by becoming completely engaged in our work in order to achieve the goal we have set for ourselves.

As far as self-efficacy is concerned, it is through action and through facing challenges in a progressive and sustained fashion that it is reinforced, away from situations that are far below or excessively beyond our abilities. A climber who dreams of one day scaling Everest has to begin by climbing smaller mountains. If he prepares himself by walking just a very short distance every day, however, he may not be training properly. The situations we place ourselves in have to be demanding but still within our reach.

Taking action in the face of this type of obstacle is mainly stepping out; taking up leadership challenges of progressive difficulty, from clarifying goals and objectives to leading a meeting, a team, or a project; taking up leadership responsibilities on a grander scale. See table 2.1 for a list of leadership roles and behaviors. At the end of the day, look also at progress made.

Weak Resilience

Sometimes, we might refuse to take action to follow a personal and collective vision that involves difficulties, obstacles, and criticism, for fear of not having the inner resources to face the inherent difficulties of this path. However, refusing to face difficulties is far more damaging than facing them, as the action itself—more often than not—provides us with the combativeness we require in order to succeed.

Developing resilience by learning to face all kinds of adversity increases our propensity to take action. What is more, situations or activities that had initially seemed problematic gradually become less and less troublesome as a result of this process, and can even end up being viewed as interesting challenges. What was a dramatic challenge yesterday might be seen tomorrow as trivial. But again the best remedy lies in actions progressively and continuously taken toward achieving a mobilizing goal, increasing your resilience along the way (see also chapter 4).

Self-Victimization

Taking action toward the achievement of our individual and collective goals demands a certain amount of work and involves certain challenges and risks. Sometimes, we might be inclined, either consciously or subconsciously, to avoid coming to terms with ourselves and refuse to assume responsibility for who we are and what we could become. Instead, we place the blame on difficult circumstances, nonunderstanding parents, managers, bad luck, or even age.

One way of coping with these obstacles is to learn to accept ourselves completely, with our strengths, weaknesses, and aspirations. Self-acceptance requires that we take charge of our life, not placing the responsibility for it on other people, circumstances, luck, or age, and not procrastinating or deferring action until a later date.

Being responsible for our own life requires the fundamental belief that no one else is responsible for our current or future situation; no one else is living our life but us. This fundamental belief brings with it a level of independence, an autonomy that comes from making our own decisions freely, taking action in various situations, being fully aware of the choices we take, and answering to ourselves rather than to others, both for the decisions we make and for our actions and their consequences—in short, it allows the emergence and sharing of our leadership capital, instead of the passive wait for a heroic leader to come along and solve all of our problems.

Idolization of Leaders and the Sense of Our Own Imperfection

The idealized image of a leader can cause a state of passiveness, even paralysis. In fact, if we could hear some people's thoughts, they would sound something like this: "She is not a charismatic leader," implying that one cannot be mobilized by this leader, or "Not being a born leader, I can't pretend to act as a one," or even "I can't take on a project like that; I'd never be as strong or capable as this extraordinary leader." In short, this idealistic view of leaders acts as a barrier as it gives us the impression that we are incapable of achieving this ideal standard, given what we see as our current limitations. Accepting ourselves is the best remedy to this obstacle to action.

Katharine Graham (1917–2001) decided at a crucial moment in her personal history that she should take over her family business—the *Washington Post*. She explains in her autobiography (Graham, 1997) that as a young adult, shy and lacking in self-assurance, she had no clear aspirations other than to adapt to whatever situations she found herself in. Her father, a rich businessman, owned a small regional newspaper, the *Wash-*

ington Post, whose running he had entrusted to Phil Graham (Katharine's husband), also a political advisor in Washington. The latter, however, suffered from severe depression despite being a brilliant and charismatic man. Katharine was entirely dependent on her husband, and had always believed that she would be nothing without him. A manic-depressive, he committed suicide in 1963.

Despite overestimating her view of her husband's management skills and having very little confidence in her own abilities, she was nevertheless determined to retain the family business. She took control of the business at age 46, telling herself that despite everything she was the only person who could do it and that she would do it her own way without pretending to be anyone else, least of all her departed husband: "I had come to realize that I could only do the job in whatever way I could do it. I couldn't try to be someone else, least of all Phil" (p. 341). This decision was the beginning of a progression in her leadership, which grew stronger and stronger with action. For Graham, the decision to take over the running of the *Washington Post* and *Newsweek* also meant recognizing her own inexperience and dedicating herself to learning the many facets of management and of the journalism industry, a task she worked on relentlessly.

The path to realizing a personal vision or goal is certainly littered with pitfalls and mistakes. Accepting our own mistakes and imperfections is one way of dealing with this situation. You are the leader of the situation in which you find yourself: head of family, teacher, team leader, supervisor, manager, or director. After all, doesn't making a mistake give you the chance to learn from it and to do better in the future?

Learning from Experiences

At a very early stage, aspiring leaders benefit from exposure to all kinds of experiences. Leadership self-efficacy can only be strengthened by these experiences. On the other hand, experiences will have no or not much of an impact on our leadership capacity without being accompanied by periods in which we reflect on them. Experience and reflection need to go hand in hand to reinforce our leadership capacity and the development of self-knowledge and self-acceptance. All experiences can strengthen our leadership capacity. This section presents how to make the most of your experiences through quality reflection.

Three types of reflection can enrich our experiences: reflection in anticipation of action, reflection in action, and reflection on action. The following strategies are inspired by Cowan's (1997) teaching students how to think.

1. Anticipatory reflection, or reflection prior to an experience helps to identify the lessons we should be looking to learn before a given experience takes place; this reflection lays the foundations for reflection in action and reflection on action.

2. Reflection in action happens quickly and is mainly concerned with problem solving and decision making. Although it is important, it is less influential than the other forms of reflection.

3. Reflection on action happens after action has taken place and attempts to draw the main lessons from it. It is primarily concerned with reflection on the strategies employed and their consequences. A greater amount of learning results not only from reflection on the strategies themselves but also on their underlying principles and values. A mentor's input can be priceless in this second level of self-reflection and learning.

These three forms of reflection help us to sort through our experiences, reflect on them from various viewpoints, take on board the lessons learned, and form personal theories that can then be used to solve problems and make future decisions. Experiences and reflections can be significantly enriched through sharing with others, such as parents, teachers, trainers, colleagues, immediate superiors, partners, mentors, or coaches. Exchanges with learning tutors provide us with an endless source of discoveries.

In order for our encounters with learning tutors to be meaningful, however, it is essential that we also know how to listen and communicate. As Plutarch (46–120) said, listening is the single most necessary element of all learning; and good hearing (listening) is the organ of wisdom, along with the willingness to ask the right questions of the right people and at the right times. By sharing, we expose ourselves to change and development as ideas, once expressed, can be either strengthened or weakened through contact with others.

Finally, several lines of action are proposed below to help you realize your unique leadership potential, for your own good as well as for collective benefits:

- Set out an action plan for realizing your aspirations, even if it is incomplete at first.
- Identify barriers and obstacles that prevent you from realizing your aspirations.
- Identify steps that you can take to clear up problem areas and remove barriers, limits, and weaknesses that hold you back from showing leadership, achieving all you can, and becoming what you want to.
- Share this personal plan with different people to gain feedback on it.
- Further develop the skills you will need to realize your aspirations.
- Use your talents and personal and collective goals wisely, helping those who stand to benefit from them. To support this strategy, place yourself in positions and organizations where your talents and skills could be useful and could be developed further.
- If you do not yet have an idea of your aspirations, nevertheless, get into the ongoing movement of leadership actions by
  - Voicing your opinions, ideas, and points of view, even if other people don't agree with you.
  - Taking up challenges and opportunities that present themselves on your path.
  - Clarifying teams' or groups' purpose and objectives.
  - Volunteering yourself as much as you can. This will provide you with more and more challenging assignments and leadership development opportunities.

CONCLUSION

In conclusion, taking action and committing yourself to being proactive are central to leadership capital actualization. This actualization could even develop into an optimal experience that is in some way related to a certain form of happiness.

Conclusion

It is our duty as human beings to proceed as though the limits of our
capabilities do not exist. — Teilhard de Chardin

The model presented in this book is based on three fundamental principles. The first of these is that each and every one of us has inside a
certain amount of leadership capital, and that this can be actualized and
used effectively. Clearly, some individuals have a greater level of this
capital than others, but the important point is that everyone has the ability to develop his or her own potential to the utmost. As leadership itself
comes in many forms, it can therefore manifest in a number of different
ways, whether in providing motivation and initiatives, influencing the
direction of a group, coming up with different viewpoints and solutions
to problems, motivating colleagues or partners, planning new methods,
developing a program, or being entrepreneurial or innovative.

The second founding principle is that we can systematically achieve the
actualization of leadership capital by deploying the seven key strategies
set out in this model. Are there strategies that are more important than
others, and thus more likely to provoke the emergence of leadership?
Personal vision and the targeting of our actions toward the goals we have
set ourselves are, without a doubt, the most powerful catalysts for this
emergence of leadership capital, as it is through the pursuit of an ideal or
a project that individuals are able to make full use of the resources at their
disposal and overcome their flaws.

In fact, the desire to achieve a goal in line with their personal vision causes individuals to put aside their tendency toward conformism, to dedicate themselves wholeheartedly to their project, to develop resilience in the face of obstacles, and to establish contact with people who will provide them with advice and support (leadership developers). All of this will allow them to gain levels of confidence and self-efficacy that they would never have suspected themselves capable of previously. However, the development of this vision and ability to act are themselves a result of the other five core strategies.

Learning that you should not always blend in with your group, developing your own self-efficacy by showing leadership, adopting a T approach to learning, developing your resilience, and establishing relationships with important individuals—all of these actions will, over time and through different experiences and personal encounters, help you to become aware of your individual and collective aspirations and the actions required to realize them. The relative importance of these seven dimensions will therefore vary according to your stage of development and current situation. The combination of these seven dimensions will also create a synergy that leads to the acceleration of leadership actualization.

The third founding element of the model proposed in this book is the idea that the learning and emergence of leadership are, first and foremost, benefits in and of themselves. In the course of my work both in teaching and consultancy, I have had the opportunity to meet with and discuss this subject with a number of business leaders, professionals, office workers, managers, and many students. What has emerged from these discussions is that those who consistently adopt an attitude of active engagement have a greater sense of well-being (both physical and psychological) than those who wait passively for their lives to unfold and who live according to the decisions and direction of others.

Every study in this area has reached a similar conclusion. Engaged individuals have more energy, are more dynamic, and take more pleasure in their work than passive individuals, who are often unsatisfied and feel a sense of victimization in their relationships with those around them. The actualization of leadership capital allows you to take control of the course of your own life by exercising careful control over situations rather than remaining passive and waiting for others, such as the all too rare "hero" leader, to come along and take matters in hand.

The emergence of your leadership benefits you and all of those to whom these acts of leadership bring hope and solutions. Modern society is in increasing need of individuals capable of exercising leadership at every level of its organizations and groups. This is the very essence of shared leadership. The model for learning leadership presented in this book, therefore, offers an alternative perspective to that of the "hero" leader, perceived as having exceptional talents and characteristics. The belief that leadership is the sole preserve of individuals in positions of authority is both utopian and dangerous.

This model, therefore, draws its inspiration from ordinary people who, day by day, through the opportunities that came their way, acted as they thought best in their own environment at both an individual and a collective level. In this way, these individuals were able to make a genuine contribution to the well-being of their society. And every one of us can achieve similar paths by becoming who we are.

References

Academy of Achievement (1995). *Standing up for freedom.* Retrieved July 24, 2008, from www.achievement.org/autodoc/page/par0int-2#par0-001

AREVA (2008). *AREVA, 2007 annual results.* Retrieved March 4, 2008, from www.areva.com/servlet/group/profile/key_figures-en.html

Ashkenas, R., Ulrich, D., Jick, T., & Kerr, S. (2002). *The boundaryless organization: Breaking the chains of organizational structure.* San Francisco: Jossey-Bass.

Avolio, B. J., Jung, D., Murry, W., & Sivasubramanian, N. (1996). Building highly developed teams: Focusing on shared leadership process, efficacy, trust and performance. In M. M. Beyerlein, D. A. Johnson, & S. T. Beyerlein (Eds.), *Advances in interdisciplinary studies of work teams* (pp. 173–209). Greenwich, CT: JAI Press.

Bandura, A. (1977). *Social learning theory.* Englewood Cliffs, NJ: Prentice-Hall.

Bandura, A. (1986). *Social foundations of thought and action: A social cognitive theory.* Englewood Cliffs, NJ: Prentice-Hall.

Bandura, A. (1997). *Self-efficacy: The exercise of control.* New York: Freeman.

Bass, B. M. (1990). *Bass & Stogdill's handbook of leadership, theory, research & managerial applications* (3rd ed.). New York: Free Press.

Benimadhu, P. P., & Gibson, J. (1999). *Leadership for tomorrow: A challenge for business today.* Ottawa: Conference Board of Canada.

Bennis, W., & Heenan, D. (1999). *Co-leaders: The power of great partnerships.* San Francisco: John Wiley & Sons.

Bennis, W., & Thomas, R. J. (2002). Crucibles of leadership. *Harvard Business Review, 80*, 39–45.

Bonterms, C. (2001). *Mariage-mariages*. Paris: Presses Universitaires de France.

Brooks, R., & Goldstein, S. (2003). *The power of resilience: Achieving balance, confidence and personal strength in your life*. New York: McGraw-Hill.

Churchill, W. S. (2003). *Never give in. The best of Winston Churchill's speeches selected by his grandson*. New York: Hyperion.

Clarke, A., & Clarke, A. (2003). *Human resilience, a fifty year quest*. New York: Jessica Kinsley.

Collins, J. (2003). The 10 greatest CEOs of all time, learn from them. *Fortune, 148*, 55–68.

Conger, J., & Pearce, C. (2003). A landscape of opportunities. In C. Pearce & J. Conger (Eds.), *Shared leadership, reframing the hows and whys of leadership* (pp. 285–304). Thousand Oaks, CA: Sage.

Coutu, D. (2002). How resilience works. *Harvard Business Review, 80*, 46–55.

Cowan, J. (1997). Teaching science for tertiary students II: Learning how to think like an engineer. In L. Jolly (Ed.), *Challenging hegemony: Reflections on reflection*. Retrieved August 1, 2008, from www.tedi.uq.edu.au/conferences/teach_conference99/papers/Jolly.html

Csikszentmihalyi, M. (1990). *Flow: The psychology of optimal experience*. New York: Harper & Row.

Cyrulnik, B. (2003). *Le murmure des fantômes*. Paris: Odile Jacob.

Devillard, O. (2001). *Coacher. Efficacité personnelle et performance collective*. Paris: Dunod.

de Vries, M. K. (2001). *The leadership mystique: A user's manual for the human enterprise*. London: Prentice Hall.

Doctors of the World. (2007). Jonathan Mann, international health and human rights pioneer. *Doctors of the World*. Retrieved July 28, 2008, from www .dowusa.org/news/feature-stories/detail/jonathan-mann

Drath, W. H. (1998). Approaching the future of leadership development. In C. D. McCauley, R. Moxley, & E. Van Velsor (Eds.), *Handbook of leadership development* (pp. 403–432). San Francisco: Jossey-Bass & The Center for Creative Leadership.

Edmonds, R. (1982). Programs of school improvement: An overview. *Educational Leadership, 4*, 4–11.

Erikson, E. (1993). *Childhood and society: The landmark work on the social significance of childhood* (rev. ed.). New York: W. W. Norton.

Fee, E., & Parry, M. (2008). Jonathan Mann, HIV/AIDS, and human rights. *Journal of Public Health Policy, 29*, 54–71. Retrieved July 28, 2008, from www .palgrave-journals.com/jphp/journal/v29/n1/full/3200160a.html

Fisher, L. (1962). *The essential Gandhi*. New York: Random House.

Fletcher, J., & Käufer, K. (2003). Shared leadership, paradox and possibility. In C. L. Pearce & J. A. Conger (Eds.), *Shared leadership, reframing the hows and whys of leadership* (pp. 21–47). Thousand Oaks, CA: Sage.

Frankl, V. (1984). *Man's search for meaning.* New York: Washington Square Press, Pocket Books.

Friedman, T. (2005). *The world is flat, a brief history of the twenty-first century.* New York: Farrar, Straus and Giroux.

Fullan, M. (2006). *Turnaround leadership.* San Francisco: Jossey-Bass.

Gardner, J. W. (1990). *On leadership.* New York: Free Press.

Girard, M. (2004, May 9). RONA. *La Presse*, business section.

Giuliani, R. (2002). *Leadership.* New York: Miramax Body.

Global Power 50. (2005) *Fortune.* Retrieved August 5 2008, from http://money .cnn.com/magazines/fortune/fortune_archive/2005/11/14/8360704/index.ht

Graham, K. (1997). *Personal history.* New York: Alfred A. Knopf.

Greenhaw, W. (2005, October 25). Parks felt "determination cover my body like a quilt." *CNN.* Retrieved July 28, 2008, from www.cnn.com/2005/US/10/25/ parks.greenhaw/index.html

Grovewell LLC. (2005). *Introduction to the GLOBE research project on leadership worldwide.* Retrieved July 28, 2008, from www.grovewell.com/ pub-GLOBE-intro.html

Gully, S. M., Incalcaterra, K. A., Joshi, A., & Beaubien, J. M. (2002). A meta-analysis of team efficacy, potency, and performance: Interdependence and level of analysis as moderators of observed relationships. *Journal of Applied Psychology, 87*, 819–832.

Hilts, P. (1998, September 4). Jonathan Mann, AIDS pioneer, is dead at 51. *New York Times.* Retrieved July 28, 2008, from http://query.nytimes.com/gst/ fullpage.html?res=9D0DE2D91E3FF937A3575AC0A96E958260

House, R., Hanges, P., Javidan, M., Dorfman, P., & Gutpa, V. (2004). *Culture, leadership, and organizations: The GLOBE study of 62 societies.* Thousand Oaks, CA: Sage.

House, R., Ruiz-Quintanilla, A., Dorfman, P., Javidan, M., Dickson, M., & Gutpa, V. (2002). *Cultural influences on leadership and organizations: Project Globe.* Retrieved July 28, 2008 from www.thunderbird.edu/wwwfiles/ms/ globe/Links/process.pdf

Joiner, B., & Josephs, S. (2007). *Leadership agility: Five levels of mastery for anticipating and initiating change.* San Francisco: Jossey-Bass.

Kellogg Foundation (2007a). *The collective leadership framework: A workbook for cultivating and sustaining community change.* Retrieved July 28, 2008, from www.ethicalleadership.org/publications/Collective%20Leadership%20 Framework%20workbook.pdf

Kellogg Foundation (2007b). *Philanthropy in the spirit of our times: 2007 annual report.* Retrieved July 28 2008, from www.wkkf.org/Pubs/AnnualReport/2007/AR2007_FullReport.pdf

Killian, B. (2004). Risk and resilience. In R. Pharoah (Ed.), *A generation at risk? HIV/AIDS, vulnerable children and security in Southern Africa* (pp. 33–63). Retrieved July 29, 2008, from www.iss.co.za/pubs/Monographs/No109/Contents.htm

Kiviat, B. (2000). The social side of schooling. *John Hopkins Magazine.* Retrieved July 28, 2008, from www.jhu.edu/~jhumag/0400web/18.html

Lezotte, L. (2002). *Revolutionary and evolutionary: The effective school movement.* Retrieved, August 4, 2008, from ali.apple.com/ali_media/Users/1000059/files/others/lezotte_article.pdf

Lieberman, A., & Miller, L. (2004). *Teacher leadership.* San Francisco: John Wiley & Sons.

Linton, R. (1955). *The tree of culture.* New York: Alfred Knopf.

Little, W., Fowler, H. W., & Coulson, J. (1955). *Oxford universal dictionary on historical principles.* London: Oxford University Press.

MacDonald, L. (2001). *The Bombardier story, planes, trains and snowmobiles.* Toronto: John Wiley & Sons.

Martel, C. (2002). *Les décisions absurdes et persistantes.* Paris: Éditions Gallimard.

McCormick (2001). Self-efficacy and leadership effectiveness: Applying social cognitive theory to leadership. *Journal of Leadership & Organizational Studies, 8,* 22–33.

Mintzberg, H. (2004, January 17). Managers, not MBAs. Speech made at a conference at the Centre Interuniversitaire de Recherche en Analyse des Organisations (CIRANO), Montreal.

Moen, P., & Erickson, M. A. (1995). Linked lives: A transgenerational approach to resilience. In P. Moen, G. H. Elder Jr., & K. Lusher (Eds.), *Examining lives in context: Perspectives on the ecology of human development* (pp. 169–207). Washington, DC: American Psychological Association.

NobelPrize.org (2008). *All Nobel Peace Prize laureates.* Retrieved August 5, 2008, from www.nobelprize.org/nobel_prizes/peace/laureates/1976/index.html

Northouse, P. (2004). *Leadership theory and practice* (3rd ed.). Thousands Oaks, CA: Sage.

Nucor, Inc. (2008). *Our mission.* Retrieved July 31, 2008, from www.nucor.com/indexinner.aspx?finpage=aboutus

Parks, R., & Haskins, J. (1992). *Rosa Parks: My story.* New York: Puffin Books.

Pearce, C. L., & Conger, J. A. (2003). All those years ago: The historical un-
derpinnings of shared leadership. In C. Pearce & J. A. Conger (Eds.), *Shared
leadership, reframing the hows and whys of leadership*. San Francisco: Sage.

Pepin, J. (1998, December 7). Ray Kroc. *Time*. Retrieved August 1, 2008, from
www.time.com/time/time100/builder/profile/kroc.html

Perlow, L., & Williams, S. (2003). Is silence killing your company? *Harvard
Business Review, 81,* 53–57.

Reivich, K., & Shatté, A. (2002). *The resilience factor*. New York: Broadway
Books.

Roberts, A. (1999). Homer's Mentor duties fulfilled or misconstrued? *History of
Education Society Journal, 64,* 81–90. Retrieved July 31, 2008, from home.att
.net/~nickols/homers_mentor.htm

Roberts, A. (2000). Mentor revisited: A phenomenological reading of the literature. *Mentoring & Tutoring, 8,* 145–170.

Roosevelt, E. (1960). *You learn by living: Eleven keys for a more fulfilling life*.
New York: Harper.

Roosevelt, F. D. (1933). *First inaugural address, March 4, 1933*. Retrieved July
28, 2008, from www.bartleby.com/124/pres.49.htlm

Rotter, J. B. (1966). Generalized expectancies for internal versus external control
of reinforcement. *Psychological Monographs, 80,* 1–28.

Rotter, J. B. (1975). Some problems and misconceptions related to the construct
of internal versus external control of reinforcement. *Journal of Consulting and
Clinical Psychology, 43,* 56–67.

Rutter, M. (1999). Resilience concepts and findings: Implications for family
therapy. *Journal of Family Therapy, 21,* 119–144.

Seers, A. (1996). Better leadership through chemistry: Toward a model of shared
team leadership. In M. M. Beyerlein, D. A. Johnson, & S. T. Beyerlein (Eds.),
Advances in interdisciplinary studies of work teams (pp. 145–172). Greenwich,
CT: JAI Press.

Senge, P. (1990). *The fifth discipline: The art and practice of the learning organization*. New York: Doubleday-Currency.

Shipp, E. R. (2005, October 25). Rosa Parks, 92, founding symbol of civil rights
movement, dies. *New York Times*. Retrieved July 23, 2008, from aad.english.
ucsb.edu/docs/10-25-05shipp.htm

Smith, K. L., & Zepp, I. G., Jr. (1974). *Search for the beloved community:
The thinking of Martin Luther King Jr.* Retrieved May 11, 2008, from www
.religion-online.org/showarticle.asp?title=1603

Sulkowicz, K. J. (2004). Worse than enemies: The CEO's destructive confidant.
Harvard Business Review, 82, 65–71.

Welch, J. (2001). *Jack, straight from the gut.* New York: Warner Books.

Werner, E., & Smith, R. S. (1989). *Vulnerable but invincible: A longitudinal study of resilient children and youth.* New York: Adams, Bannister & Cox.

Werner, E. E., & Smith, R. S. (1992). *Overcoming the odds: High risk children from birth to adulthood.* Ithaca, NY: Cornell University Press.

Zullow, H. M., Oettingen, G., Peterson, C., & Seligman, M. E. F. (1988). Pessimistic explanatory in the historical record: CAVing LBJ, presidential candidates, and East Versus West Berlin. *American Psychologist, 43,* 673–682.